"Life as it had been would ne

Those pain-filled words come fr
MW01236237

My Time to Grieve. She knows fr... experience that we each have times in our lives when we grieve over one or many losses. She knows firsthand that grieving is necessary and a process. Can we reach the other side of grief to a brighter day? Can we let go? Blame God? Or trust Him? Can we reach out to others who are grieving?

Her book has the answer to those and many questions and incorporates her own message of hope for hurting hearts.

—YVONNE LEHMAN, director of Blue Ridge "Summer" and "Autumn" novel retreats and author of fifty novels. Her latest release is *Aloha Brides,* a collection of historical novels set in Hawaii.

Phoebe Leggett is a shining example of one who is able to comfort just as she herself has been comforted (2 Corinthians 1:4). I know, because I've seen it not only in her written words, but in her life. She exudes a solid faith and an unyielding peace that comes only from journeying to the deepest places of grief and finding God there. Now, through her writing, her poetry, and her insights, she walks beside you on your own journey through grief, encouraging and supporting you every step of the way.

—ANN TATLOCK, award-winning novelist

Some people go places others only dream of going. But others have to go *through* places that, for most, are simply nightmares. Phoebe Leggett speaks of traveling through such a place and yet finds help and healing in the darkest of valleys as she walks with the Good Shepherd. In *It's My Time to Grieve,* she shares her source of strength with hurting souls, not simply from head knowledge, but from a heart that has lived it.

—JERRY D. MADDEN, Senior Pastor, Praise Cathedral

It's My Time To Grieve

A Journey into Grief and Back

Phoebe Leggett

CROSSBOOKS
PUBLISHING

CrossBooks™
A Division of LifeWay
1663 Liberty Drive
Bloomington, IN 47403
www.crossbooks.com
Phone: 1-866-879-0502

First published by CrossBooks: 11/01/2011

ISBN: 978-1-4627-0622-8 (sc)
ISBN: 978-1-4627-0623-5 (hc)
ISBN: 978-1-4627-1124-6 (e)

Library of Congress Control Number: 2011916374

Printed in the United States of America

This book is printed on acid-free paper.

To Cathy Pendola

"Grieve, mourn, and wail. Change your laughter to mourning and your joy to gloom" (James 4:9).

CONTENTS

FOREWORD

By
Vonda Skelton
It's My Time to Grieve

On Mother's Day 1994, I ended the day as always after a family gathering—spending one-on-one time with my daddy. We talked about his health issues and possible surgery, the first book I was still trying to get published, and the ongoing issues with my brother. Our final words were words of affirmation and love.

Twelve days later, he was dead.

My life was forever changed that day. Although it's expected that parents will die first and leave their children, I wasn't prepared for the smothering grief that moved in and took over my life.

I had only a few moments to respond to the shock of his death before taking my assigned position as the firstborn. I became the parent as I took over for my mom, answering questions and making decisions on her behalf. My husband and I left the hospital with her, stopped by my parents' home, and grabbed what we needed. She would be staying with us for a while.

I helped her plan the funeral and complete the obituary; I took her shopping and bought her funeral dress; I managed the register of food, gifts, and condolences.

The day after the funeral, while writing the obligatory thank-you notes, I crashed. I ran outside and screamed at the world. How could people go on as if nothing had ever happened? How could they go to work, buy groceries, and cut grass? My daddy was dead! Didn't anybody care?

Three weeks later, I was at the dentist, sitting in the exam chair, waiting for the doctor. I closed my eyes to the pain and tried again to get a handle on my emotions. "Slow breaths, in and out," I reminded myself. "It's been three weeks, for crying out loud." I opened my eyes and gazed out the picture window . . . and broke down.

There, right in front of me, was a massive oak tree, split in two. The right half was green and vibrant, ready for the next adventure in life. The left was a lifeless brown, struck down by some unexpected force, its barren limbs declaring its demise.

And it hit me: I was the tree.

The world told me I had simply experienced the natural chain of life. It told me I should be thankful that my daddy had died suddenly and had not suffered. It told me time was up, and I needed to move on.

But I was the tree. Half of me was green and growing and doing everything possible to enjoy the next adventure in life. But the other half of me was dead, my broken heart declaring that life as I had known it was gone.

The dentist came in, saw me crying, and assumed I was fearful of the procedure. I wish it had been that simple.

To this day, I sometimes still struggle with the loss of my daddy. I cry for the fact that he never got to meet my grandchildren or see my books in print. I cry because he never sat in an audience and heard me speak or watched me bring tears of joy and laughter to those who listened. I cry because I miss his funny stories, his crazy antics, and his loving words.

But even though I still cry, I've found a way to feel the joy of his presence: I keep my daddy alive through my books. Remember that first manuscript I couldn't get published for so long? It was written five months before Daddy died, a mystery for boys and girls, somewhat based on my family's vacation to Tybee Island, Georgia, when I was a child. Yes, I'm my main character, Bitsy, and her family is my family. Her daddy is my daddy.

His funny stories, crazy antics, and loving words come alive on the pages of my books, entertaining both kids and adults. He brings tears of joy and laughter to the eyes of my readers. And sometimes, he brings tears of emotion through the heartfelt, real-life moments my daddy and I shared . . . that are now shared by Bitsy and her dad.

It's been a healing process.

You could do the same thing through *It's My Time to Grieve.* By giving the guidance, the freedom, and the place, Phoebe allows you the opportunity to remember—and write about—those moments. Those times your loved one made you laugh and the times he or she drove you crazy. The chance to remember and write can be the key to progressing through the steps of grief, rather than struggling in a mire of sadness and regret.

Perhaps your words won't come out as fiction, written for the entertainment of others. Maybe they'll be secret words, written only to verbalize the pain, settle the conflict, or applaud the life. But whatever they are, they can still be words of healing. After all, every one of us needs a time—and a way—to heal. *It's My Time to Grieve* can give you exactly what you need.

I pray for God's healing touch as you read through the pages of this book.

—VONDA SKELTON, Speaker and Author of *Seeing Through the Lies: Unmasking the Myths Women Believe* and *The Bitsy Burroughs Mysteries* - www.VondaSkelton.com

PREFACE

When my twenty-two-year-old son was killed in a car crash in 2004, I did not know what to do. I had never experienced such devastation in my entire life. The confusion, the shock, and the disbelief were overwhelming as I struggled to grasp the reality of what had just happened.

At that moment I decided to keep a record of my journey, not realizing God had a plan to use my loss as reinforcement for others who are also brokenhearted. And, by writing this book, my journey through grief has a destination.

—PHOEBE LEGGETT

ACKNOWLEDGMENTS

A Special Thanks to:

Ann Tatlock, for guiding me into the world of professional writing. Ann is a personal friend and one of my first mentors. Our friendship began when my friend Bonnie introduced us at a Women's Bible Study at Billy Graham's *The Cove* located in Asheville, North Carolina. Because of this introduction, Ann invited me to the Blue Ridge Mountain's Christian Writer's Conference in Ridgecrest, North Carolina. This conference and several more, coupled with Ann's confidence in my work, gave me the assurance I needed to pursue the writing of this book on grief. Our friendship is ongoing and a testimony to how God works out the details of our lives through others.

Bonnie Lowdermilk, now deceased, was my best friend from childhood until her death in 2007. Her encouragement helped push me into a writing career when she introduced me to her friend Ann Tatlock.

Brian Foley, my middle child and oldest son, for his willingness to write about his feelings of remorse following the death of his sibling and for his assistance in helping me recall childhood antics of his brother Matthew. Several memories inspired personal stories that are scattered throughout the pages of *It's My Time to Grieve.*

Carolyn K. Knefely for her friendship and willingness to write her story in *It's My Time to Grieve* about the infant daughter she lost years ago. Her narrative offers hope and healing to others who have lost a baby in death.

Cathy Pendola, for her willingness to write her story that details the tragic loss her son Dominic. We met online through a mutual friend of a friend shortly after the death of her son. Matt had been dead about three months when we began our e-mail communication. Our online friendship has continued for over seven years. Together we worked through much of the grieving process. She remains a solid rock for me. Her stories are dynamic and heartfelt.

Cindy Sproles is a personal friend who continues to inspire many by providing daily devotionals on *www.ChristianDevotions.us,* a website she created for the Internet. Cindy's devotional *Bring Them Home* is included in *It's My Time to Grieve* and has great meaning in an essential chapter.

Dana Leggett, my husband for over twenty-two years, stepfather to my children, and a great supporter of my writing craft. His love, sensitivity, and assistance provided ongoing support for the writing of *It's My Time to Grieve.*

Edie Melson for her strict but solid instruction of basic writing skills that reinforced a good work ethic and continuous desire to achieve my God-given purpose for writing. Edie is a personal friend and expert editor.

Leigh Ann, a personal friend, for her willingness to write about losing her nephew in a car crash, and the tragic effect it had on her family.

Lori Marett, who took the time to edit my manuscript, suggest placement of chapters, and offer ideas to further develop the content of *It's My Time to Grieve.* Her contributed stories provide valid points and profound insight. Her belief that I could accomplish this work was one of the catalysts that spurred me forward. Lori is a personal friend and expert editor.

Randy Stone, Pastor of Meadowbrook Free Will Baptist Church in Black Mountain, North Carolina, for his constant support and lasting friendship that blessed our family following the death of my son and my mother.

Belle Woods, a personal friend and devoted Christian. Her willingness to write about the death of her husband provides significant insight in *It's My Time to Grieve.* Her devotion to the memory of her husband will relate to others who have also lost a spouse through death.

Vonda Skelton, a personal friend who encouraged me to pursue the difficult task of writing *It's My Time to Grieve.* After she critiqued my first draft, she said I would have to re-live the pain of the past in order to write about it. Her advice was honest and was the only way I could have achieved my desired objective, which is to help others. Her support pushed me forward as I struggled to re-live the terrifying events of my son's tragic death. Her friendship, solid writing instruction, and Christian character continue to inspire me toward greater writing goals.

Yvonne Lehman, one of my first mentors who drew me into a fold of writers through her support group. She critiqued many of my stories while encouraging me to pursue publication. Her friendship and support will always be appreciated.

INTRODUCTION

Life Beyond Foliage

"There is hope for a tree: If it is cut down, it will sprout again, and its new shoots will not fail" (Job 14:7).

"Here, Mom, these are for you." Grinning from ear to ear, my vivacious teenage son shoved a dish garden full of tiny shriveled plants into my hands. "The store manager threw them away," he said. "I thought you might want them."

The plants were so withered I had serious doubts they would survive. But Matt had given them to me, so I drenched them with water and hoped for the best. To my amazement, and his delight, a little attention triggered those dying plants to sprout new leaves. Vibrant foliage was soon growing from all five. Each day those lush, colorful leaves filled my kitchen with the freshness of life.

Over time, the plants were transplanted into separate containers as their growth extended well beyond the small bowl that held them.

Many years have passed since those special plants were given to me. A vast amount of tears have streamed beneath life's bridge. Matthew was killed in a car crash over seven years ago. But most of the plants that he had insisted I take are still alive, and growing. When I look at the fullness of their beauty, I realize my son continues to exist. And there is hope for our reunion because life never ends. It just transplants to another place.

CHAPTER ONE

Losing My Son

A piercing shrill jarred me into a semiconscious state as my mind struggled to comprehend the reason for my rude awakening. Had the thing I'd always dreaded just happened? The atmosphere in the room was charged.

Illumination from a digital clock on the nightstand registered the time at half past one. The muffled drone of my husband's voice filtered past my ear as he sat, stiff and rigid, on the side of the bed.

So this was the reason for my premature stirring.

I bolted upright and saw the color drain from Dana's face. The jarring blast of the telephone and his uneasy manner triggered an indigestible fear that plunged me headlong into an unbelievable sequence of terrorizing events.

He patted my shoulder in a comforting way as he handed me the phone. I grabbed it, shaken and confused; an unbelievable fear playing havoc with my senses.

"Mom . . . Mom." The sound of my daughter's strangled voice pierced my heart. My mind went limp. "Matt . . . Matthew's dead." Her words were raw.

"What?" The beat of my heart accelerated. I thought it would explode.

Her message continued through congested sobs and staggered hiccups. "He's dead—killed in a car crash—his car—by himself—the hospital—ambulance . . .

Stark silence echoed through the room.

"Mom . . . Mom . . . Hello?"

"I . . . I don't believe it." My mind froze, not wanting to understand, not wanting to hear.

I grappled at her words. What had Dawn just said? Matthew's dead? I couldn't comprehend her words. *Matthew's dead . . . Matthew's dead . . .* The words tumbled over and over in my head as gut-wrenching terror swept through me. A bolt of lightning could not have been more damaging.

In just seconds, I was spiraling downward into an insidious pit of horror. Could I ever climb out of the abyss I had just fallen into?

Little by little, the unspeakable details of my twenty-two-year-old son's last moments began to emerge.

After eleven o'clock Tuesday evening, Matt had driven to the home of his cousin following his second-shift job at Food Lion, a grocery store establishment in Madison, North Carolina. But after his arrival, he made a fatal decision. Desiring a fast meal to satisfy his hunger, he decided a quick trip to Taco Bell would be short and simple.

His foot heavy on the pedal, he sped down an unfamiliar road from Stoneville to Madison amid a torrential downpour of rain. Oblivious to the sharp curve ahead that locals had dubbed Dead Man's Curve, he continued his short trek at breakneck speed. As his car slid into the long-famed curve, it hydroplaned on the slick and water-drenched pavement, and spun out of control.

Overcorrecting his mistake triggered the car to flip several times on its way down a steep embankment. The now compacted auto slammed into a huge tree that prevented a further descent into the ravine. Later his car would be documented as a total loss.

Due to the nature of the accident, Matthew's head was knocked about and began to swell. Broken ribs, shattered bones, and other injuries were sustained. And yet he was still alive.

However, following a fast ride with paramedics to the hospital, his race with life was over. The police were astonished when they learned Matt had not survived his trauma, as they recalled conversing with him while medics loaded him into the ambulance. Reports later indicated the severity of the crash had caused more internal than external injury.

Matthew had been living with relatives on his father's side over one hundred miles from where his stepfather and I lived. For that reason, and others, his aunt called my daughter instead of me when she learned of his death. However, after of the accident, unresolved issues from the past became unimportant and superficial.

I staggered from bed in a stupor, struggling to comprehend the magnitude of what I had just heard. *What could I do? What did I need to do? What did I have to do?*

Life as it had been would never be the same again.

STONEVILLE man dies in car wreck
By Gerri Hunt, News Editor of the Madison Messenger, Madison, NC

THE MESSENGER

Stoneville man dies in car wreck

By GERRI HUNT
News Editor

MAYODAN—A Stoneville man was killed Tuesday night when he lost control of his car and hit some trees at 11:20 p.m., said Tangie Holcombe, spokesperson for the N.C. State Highway Patrol.

Stephen Matthew Foley, 22, of 4000 N.C. 135, was driving South on U.S. 220 Business when he lost control of a 2001 Chevrolet as he come out of a left curve.

Foley ran off the right shoulder of the road, overcorrected, and slid around to the left, and went off the shoulder again, said Holcombe.

The car rolled down a steep embankment, where its driver's side hit a tree. The car spun, the passenger's side striking another tree.

Foley was transported to Morehead Memorial Hospital, where he later died.

Madison-Mayodan Rescue Squad member Steve Boles was at the scene.

"He was conscious and alert and talking to us," he said. "He complained of pain in his left arm and left hand."

Boles said he was surprised to hear of Foley's death.

Trooper G. S. Grissom said Foley was not wearing a seat belt and estimated that he was driving 70 in a 55 mph speed limit.

Madison and Mayodan police and fire departments also responded to the call.

Estrangement with my ex-husband's family following our divorce years earlier, and later his death, had caused a rift between the two families. But unusual situations carve out unexpected paths to bring people together again. In just minutes, I had placed a call to my former sister-in-law, my son's aunt, as details and confirmation were essential. The aunt was as hysterical as my daughter had been, reaching out to me as I was to her. Issues of the past instantly dissolved as the present crisis claimed prominence.

The details of that horrific evening have now been pieced together with information obtained from police, medical personnel, family members, and a former sister-in-law who is head nurse in a hospital emergency room. Her experience includes firsthand knowledge of catastrophic injuries similar to Matthew's. She explained in detail how his body had reacted to the accident, and the verity that comparable collisions almost always result in instant death. Somehow Matthew had not been killed at the moment of impact, but passed away later in the hospital.

According to police records, Matt tried to escape his encapsulated prison, but was unsuccessful. His crash had gone undetected for some time as the hour was late, and the weather harsh. With traffic at a minimum, the accident was concealed for longer than was normal. Later it was discovered Matt carried a handgun for protection. Although injured, he had been able to drag the weapon from its hiding place and direct a bullet through the already smashed car window, hoping to draw attention to his plight.

A couple of police officers were soon on the scene. One was Matthew's own first cousin.

"We'll get you out, buddy," he said. "Don't worry. You'll make it. We've called an ambulance."

The jaws of life were employed as medics rushed to salvage Matt from a smashed and destroyed vehicle. He was then rushed to the emergency room at Eden Memorial Hospital complaining of excruciating pain in arm and chest. The ambulance was in transit as Matthew's reacquainted relatives were alerted, and warned that time was short. They were instructed to get to the hospital as soon as possible.

Although his head was swelling, most of Matt's injuries were internal, as later documented. It was also reported, had he survived, he would have had brain damage. But it wasn't until his heart stopped beating that the hospital staff began to grasp the severity of his injuries. CPR was initiated, but to no avail. Matthew had been in a fast race with death, and death had won.

Did he realize he was taking his final breath? I do not know. What I do understand is that God granted him a few extra minutes to make his peace. Did he? Eternity alone holds the key.

The excruciating pain he reported to paramedics could have been due to broken bones or shattered bone fragments probing his heart cavity. One report indicated his heart may have been pierced with a shard of broken rib, causing a fast and brutal demise.

Family members failed to arrive in time to see Matthew before he died a short time after his arrival to the emergency room.

Police records indicated no alcohol or drugs were found in his body.

An autopsy was suggested, but what was the point. Matthew was dead. Nothing could ever change that fact.

IN MEMORY
of
Stephen Matthew Foley

Born May 10, 1982 - Died July 28, 2004

It's been a day of sadness
on my journey into grief.
Sometimes my tears would fall like rain,
yet promised no relief.

It's been a year of sadness
of brokenness and fears.
Sometimes my mind became so numb
engulfed by floods of tears.

But God has been so very close.
His Spirit hovered near.
God's promises are true,
so what have I to fear?

He promised me my children
together would be there
at that dinner in the sky,
that Jesus will prepare.

God the Father had to grieve
when His Son had to die
so I could have a hope
to see my son on high.

On this journey into grief,
my sorrow's just a part
for memories of the past
I hold within my heart.

And looking to the future
is my hope and gain.
For soon the sun will shine again,
and push away the rain.

With his shy and silly grin
my son again I'll see.
With God, and those I love,
we'll spend eternity.

By faith, I know God's word is true,
on my journey into grief.
A time to weep, a time to mourn;
and then He gives sweet peace.

©Phoebe Leggett

Coping with Death

One way I learned to cope with the death of my son was to write poetry. When feelings were raw, I scribbled them down. As memories flooded my soul, thoughts were put in written form. And when despair was my only focus, God placed words of prose into my spirit that were transferred to paper. As time moved forward, so did my desire to journal thoughts and feelings on paper. Poetry became a memorial of grief—a channel to mend my troubled heart. Without a doubt, the loss of my son was a horrible finale to all accumulated hopes and dreams.

Music of consolation played over and over again addressed my need for confirmation, assurance, and hope that a better day would emerge. Songs by Cheryl Salem, a well-known Christian vocalist who lost her daughter Gabrielle to cancer, was another anchor in my storm. Her music reaffirmed my confidence in God as I realized she understood, first hand, the harshness of death.

The staggering newness of a loss can be overwhelming and harsh. Christian music has a way of softening the rush of insanity that continues to flood the mind. Christian material on grief can also be consoling as well as informative. A recorded message from the Bible that brings comfort may also be beneficial and supportive. Del Way, a minister and recording artist, along with Andrew Wommack, President of Charis Bible College, per my request, provided recorded information on grieving a loss.

After a loved one has passed, it's helpful to find new ways of managing the bouts of sorrow and feelings of insecurity that will surface. This insanity of emotion can claim every waking moment, and is difficult to swallow. A new hobby is one way of releasing raw emotions in a positive way, as it allows a creative side to emerge. Activities such as writing, gardening, painting, or volunteering are other ways that bring healing and restoration to a shattered soul.

New interests will often reactivate a sense of worth and value. Finding a new outlet may help to lessen the amount of time needed to recover from the trauma of grief. Re-centering your thoughts can diminish new issues of sorrow that leave no sense of purpose for your life. Perhaps starting a grief ministry of your own will bring the emotional healing you need, and desire.

CHAPTER TWO

Grief

"The Lord is gracious and righteous; our God is full of compassion" (Psalm 116:5).

Grief—noun
1. keen mental suffering or distress over affliction or loss; sharp sorrow; painful regret
2. a cause or occasion of keen distress or sorrow
Synonyms: anguish, heartache, woe, misery; sadness, melancholy, moroseness.
Antonyms: grief
grief

—Synonyms
1. anguish, heartache, woe, misery; sadness, melancholy, moroseness.
See sorrow.
—Antonyms
1. joy.

At an unscheduled and unpredictable moment, death will come to call. Like an unexpected visitor, this disruption will confront and confuse your very existence. And when it arrives, deep sorrow, unbelievable anguish, and excruciating misery will overtake you as a thief in the night. "For you know very well that the day of the Lord will come like a thief in the night" (1 Thessalonians 5:2).

Death affects everyone in one way or another. It is no stranger. When I ponder the military, our heroes, losing their lives on foreign soil far from home, I shudder for their families. Although war has been reoccurring for our great country throughout its history, Americans continue to grieve their losses. Each generation has surrendered countless soldiers to battleground conflicts or war-related deaths, and the number continues to soar.

There's also a combat zone on domestic soil as children are dying far too young. Drugs, alcohol, abuse, and neglect are rampant and continue to steal the lives of our youth. Even the safety of the unborn is in jeopardy as thousands are murdered on any given day in abortion mills. This is possible as the immoral believe we live in a disposable society.

What about the parents of a child who has been abducted? Insane uncertainty, without a doubt, overtakes the mind as questions concerning the existence and whereabouts of their missing child take over. All understanding dies when parents, in anguished turmoil, contemplate the unknown: Is their child dead or alive?

Other families have lost loved ones to violence and murder. Many around us are suffering deep inside, yet their torment remains hidden. Insidious and insane predators kidnap, rape, and murder our children, or other family members, without any sense of decency or morality—allowing their lust to sacrifice the lives of the innocent. Satan is evil and causes men, and women, to do wicked things. Lacking restraint, the immoral accept his vile devices without conscience. Evidence of Satan's malevolence will continue until the end of time.

STORM

Dark storm clouds gather thick
as harsh winds whip about.
The brightest light in life
has died and flickered out.

Death's storm will never end.
Its harsh winds won't subside.
Dark clouds are always near
as memories collide.

For 'tho the time will pass
'mid flash of sun and night,
rain drops its glistening tears
in memory of the light.

2007 Award-winning poem by ©Phoebe Leggett

Death

The Bible refers to death as a sleep or being asleep. "When I awake, I am still with you" (Psalm 139:18).

Death (deth)—***noun***
The act of dying; the end of life; the total and permanent cessation of all the vital functions of an organism.
The state of being dead: *to lie still in death.*
—***Synonyms***
1. decease, demise, passing, departure.

—***Antonyms***
1. birth, life.

"Give light to my eyes, or I will **sleep in death**" (Psalm 13:3).

"Multitudes who **sleep in the dust of the earth** will awake: some to everlasting life, others to shame and everlasting contempt" (Daniel 2:2).

"We will not all **sleep**, but we will all be changed—in a flash, in the twinkling of an eye, at the last trumpet" (1 Corinthians 15:51).

"I would **be asleep** and at rest . . . " (Job 3:13)

"He went in and said to them, 'Why all this commotion and wailing? The child **is not dead** but **asleep'"** (Mark 5:39).

"For when David had served God's purpose in his own generation, he **fell asleep; he was buried** with his fathers . . . " (Acts 13:36)

"But Christ has indeed been raised from the dead, the first fruits of those who have **fallen asleep**. For since death came through a man, the resurrection of the dead comes also through a man. For as in Adam all die, so in Christ all will be made alive. But each in his own turn: Christ, the first fruits; then, when he comes, those who belong to him. Then the end will come, when he hands over the kingdom to God the Father after he has destroyed all dominion, authority and power. For he must reign until he has put all his enemies under his feet. The last enemy to be destroyed is **death**." (1 Corinthians 15:20-26).

"Brothers, we do not want you to be ignorant about those **who fall asleep**, or to grieve like the rest of men, who have no hope. We believe that Jesus died and rose again and so we believe that God will bring with Jesus those who have **fallen asleep** in him. According to the Lord's own word, we tell you that we who are still alive, who are left till the coming of the Lord, will certainly not precede those who have **fallen asleep**." (2 Thessalonians 4:13-15).

Losing a loved one in death can be the most devastating occurrence one will ever experience. Sensations of draining hopelessness will overtake a conscious mind at any undisclosed time. Unrelenting sorrow may rip into the core of everything one has always believed. Disparaging thoughts can even question the existence of God. The rawness of grief won't be defined in mere words. These harsh feelings are unlike anything ever experienced before. This uncontrollable emotion called grief can strip all innocence from life. It will zap a person's very strength with a feeling so staggering that the Bible discloses this truth in two simple words: "Jesus wept" (John 11:35). Although these words may seem trivial, for Him the emotional pain must have been staggering.

The Story of Lazarus

Jesus, our perfect example, revealed His grief by shedding tears of sorrow when His friend Lazarus died. And, for the rest of us, there's no way around the grieving process. Without option or delay, complicated or not;

when bereavement presents itself, we will go through pain and sorrow. There is no other choice.

> Now a man named Lazarus was sick. He was from Bethany, the village of Mary and her sister Martha. This Mary, whose brother Lazarus now lay sick, was the same one who poured perfume on the Lord and wiped his feet with her hair. So the sisters sent word to Jesus, "Lord, the one you love is sick."
>
> When he heard this, Jesus said, "This sickness will not end in death. No, it is for God's glory so that God's Son may be glorified through it." Jesus loved Martha and her sister and Lazarus. Yet when he heard that Lazarus was sick, he stayed where he was two more days.
>
> Then he said to his disciples, "Let us go back to Judea."
>
> "But Rabbi," they said, "a short while ago the Jews tried to stone you, and yet you are going back there?"
>
> Jesus answered, "Are there not twelve hours of daylight? A man who walks by day will not stumble, for he sees by this world's light. It is when he walks by night that he stumbles, for he has no light." After he had said this, he went on to tell them, "Our friend Lazarus has **fallen asleep**; but I am going there to wake him up."
>
> His disciples replied, "Lord, if he sleeps, he will get better." Jesus had been speaking of his **death**, but his disciples thought he meant natural sleep. So then he told them plainly, "Lazarus is dead, and for your sake I am glad I was not there, so that you may believe. But let us go to him."
>
> Then Thomas (called Didymus) said to the rest of the disciples, "Let us also go, that we may die with him."
>
> On his arrival, Jesus found that Lazarus had already been in the tomb for four days. Bethany was less than two miles from Jerusalem and many Jews had come to Martha and Mary to comfort them in the loss of their brother. When Martha heard that Jesus was coming, she went out to meet him, but Mary stayed at home.
>
> "Lord," Martha said to Jesus, "if you had been here, my brother would not have died. But I know that even now God will give you whatever you ask."
>
> Jesus said to her, "Your brother will rise again."
>
> Martha answered, "I know he will rise again in the resurrection at the last day."

Jesus said to her, "I am the resurrection and the life. **He who believes in me will live, even though he dies; and whoever lives and believes in me will never die.** Do you believe this?"

"Yes, Lord," she told him, "I believe that you are the Christ, the Son of God, who was to come into the world." And after she had said this, she went back and called her sister Mary aside. "The Teacher is here," she said, "and is asking for you." When Mary heard this, she got up quickly and went to him.

Now Jesus had not yet entered the village, but was still at the place where Martha had met him. When the Jews who had been with Mary in the house, comforting her, noticed how quickly she got up and went out, they followed her, supposing she was going to the tomb to mourn there.

When Mary reached the place where Jesus was and saw him, she fell at his feet and said, "Lord, if you had been here, my brother would not have died." When Jesus saw her weeping, and the Jews who had come along with her also weeping, he was deeply moved in spirit and troubled. "Where have you laid him?" he asked.

"Come and see, Lord," they replied.

Jesus wept.

Then the Jews said, "See how he loved him!

But some of them said, "Could not he who opened the eyes of the blind man have kept this man from dying?"

Jesus, once more deeply moved, came to the tomb. It was a cave with a stone laid across the entrance. "Take away the stone," he said.

"But, Lord," said Martha, the sister of the dead man, "by this time there is a bad odor, for he has been there four days."

Then Jesus said, "Did I not tell you that if you believed, you would see the glory of God?" So they took away the stone. Then Jesus looked up and said, "Father, I thank you that you have heard me. I knew that you always hear me, but I said this for the benefit of the people standing here, that they may believe that you sent me." When he had said this, Jesus called in a loud voice, "Lazarus, come out!" The dead man came out, his hands and feet wrapped with strips of linen, and a cloth around his face. Jesus said to them, "Take off the grave clothes and let him go" (John 11:1-44).

CHAPTER THREE

Stages of Grieving

Several stages of sorrow are experienced following the death of a loved one. Levels of mourning may differ from person to person, but the fundamental stages are normal and documented. It may help to know what to expect while going through the grieving process. Five basic steps are listed below.

- Denial: Shock and disbelief are initial feelings that follow the death of a loved one. You will feel numb and unable to believe the death is real. This stage may last for a short time, or an extended period of time. Hours and days will run together as the mind tries to process the facts of what has happened. The disbelief that's felt can become overwhelming while you struggle through this stage.

- Anger: You may become enraged and have trouble sleeping, or be unable to function at a normal pace during this stage. Anger at your loved one may surface, or anger may be expressed in a negative way toward others. This is also the time when grief can become severe. Strong disbelief that the deceased has gone away can be overwhelming, and may cause uncontrollable rage. Your anger may be kept in check, but you may experience irritation or resentment in silence.

- Regret: During this stage, extreme remorse will surface at not having been more tolerant or understanding of your loved one before they died. This is a normal reaction if there are regrets of any nature. Realizing your inability to apologize, or change the past, may cause emotional distress. This is something only time can heal. You may feel sensations of guilt for a variety of reasons. It's normal to experience emotions of remorse and regret.

- Depression: In this stage, you may become despondent and lose interest in activities, work, or life in general as emotions are sorted out following a loss. A sudden bout of crying or withdrawal from others is normal and expected. It may be difficult to forgive yourself for some reason. Or you may harbor regret that your loved one didn't live a long life. Being out of control and unable to change any of those circumstances can cause depression. If your sadness becomes overwhelming, it may be necessary to seek a medical professional for assistance through this stage.

- Acceptance: The final stage of grieving comes when one realizes their loved one has died, been buried, and is no more on this earth. It is what it is. There are no U-turns or reversals in this trauma. As sad as it is, there's nothing more that can be done to change the circumstance. Now is the time to realize you have your own life to live. As difficult as it may be, you must try to move on and accept your loved one's death as part of the cycle of life.

IT'S OVER

Tragedy not averted,
but hit head on.
Life as it was
is over and done.

Last words have been said.
Last things have been done.
That sad day is now.
I buried my son.

©Phoebe Leggett

There's never a set time to complete the basic stages of heartache. It's individually based, and depends on one's own ability to cope. Only time can heal a broken heart. And, only God can provide the necessary comfort that's needed to heal.

"My heart is broken within me; all my bones tremble" (Jeremiah 23:9).

"A broken and contrite heart, O God, you will not despise" (Psalm 51:17).

BROKE

Death broke my heart.
Like jagged stone splinters
with sharp, shattered edges
and raw broken ridges.

Death broke my heart,
Exploded like a Coke
with shards of broken glass.
And yes, it is still broke.

Denial

"Then Jesus said to his disciples, "If anyone would come after me, he must **deny** himself and take up his cross and follow me" (Matthew 16:24).

Definition of *denial*—an assertion that something said, believed, alleged, etc., is false; a disbelief in the existence or reality of a thing. The refusal to recognize or acknowledge; a disowning or disavowal: *Peter's denial of Christ.*

Psychology: an unconscious defense mechanism used to reduce anxiety by denying thoughts, feelings, or facts that are consciously intolerable.

But, why not you? The Bible explains that God is no respecter of persons. "For God does not show favoritism" (Romans 2:11).

"He causes His sun to rise on the evil and the good, and sends rain on the righteous and the unrighteous" (Matthew 5:45).

We don't know why things happen the way they do. We may feel responsible for the demise of a loved one, or blame God for an untimely death. But it's important to realize that God is in control even through we may have lost ours. His promise to be with us during our struggles in life is our only hope and strength.

Losing My Nephew

By Leah Ann

My oldest sister, Sandra, lost her firstborn son in a car wreck on Mother's Day when he was twenty-one. Another sister, Mary's, firstborn son was in the same wreck. I always call it *the wreck* instead of an automobile accident because of the wreckage it leaves in the hearts and lives of those left behind.

Sandra was called to the hospital and told her son had died. But upon arrival, she learned that her son was not the one who had died because she recognized his voice as he screamed in the emergency room. Her son lived, but Mary's son died at the scene. This accident was about twenty-five years ago. Mary is still a bitter, angry woman. Sandra has always found relief in a bottle. So does her son, the one who survived the accident. In a way, we all died that day.

Of ten children, eight of us had sons as our firstborn, one had a son as her second born, and one didn't have children at all.

There are many hurting people who don't know how to deal with grief. They need someone who knows the depth of their suffering and can to minister to them. Those of us who are fortunate enough to have raised our firstborn are called *the lucky ones.* We are locked out of the hearts of those who have suffered the ultimate loss. We're unable to reach the place that aches. In a way, we can't understand. But God never allows us to suffer without a reason.

~

With the passing of a loved one, bitterness and depression may become your reality. However, if feelings of despair settle in and remain, the time to consult a professional may be essential. There's no shame in requesting this type of help, as depression is a natural process of grieving. And the possibility of reoccurring depression could be predictable. Over time, your depressive feelings will pass, and a more positive outlook should become your position.

SORROW

It's a hurt
that won't go away.
It was here yesterday,
and it's here today.

It won't be gone,
even after tomorrow.
It has its grip.
It is called sorrow.

This painful hurt
is here to stay.
Long is the night,
and long is the day.

I can't go forward
in sorrow and pain.
The sun never shines.
There's always more rain.

Visiting the cemetery often brings a sense of connection for family and friends. For others, it will be a painful reminder that their loved one has died. This all depends on the relationship shared with the deceased. Placing memorials and flowers at the gravesite can also bring a sense of closure while demonstrating love and compassion for a deceased loved one and for others who are left to grieve.

Many times, fresh flowers and a memorial cross are left on the roadside where an accident claimed a life. Sadness may be overwhelming when viewing these special mementos, if but for a moment. Allow those feelings to surface from time to time as they are beneficial to emotional restoration. Over time, these sentiments can help bring a sense of acceptance and closure to your heart.

Acceptance

"Jesus replied, 'Not everyone can **accept** this word, but only those to whom it has been given'" (Matthew 19:11).

"Even in laughter the heart may ache, and joy may **end** in grief" (Proverbs 14:13).

Definition of *Acceptance*: The process of accepting, the act of taking or receiving something offered. The act of believing, approval, belief in something, agreement

Will I be able to accept the death of a loved one? The most understandable answer is "No." But with God's help and the healing of time, much of the bitterness caused by the death should diminish. Try to remember the positive accomplishments of the deceased, and recall joyful moments spent together. Push aside thoughts that cause hurt and pain, and begin to concentrate on memories that bring laughter and joy. By redirecting your thoughts, the constant ache of a broken heart should begin to diminish. After that, more positive recollections can become your fondest memories. These are the treasures that won't fade with the passing of time.

I don't know if my son was a Christian when he died. Was he prepared to meet his God? That unanswered question will forever remain a part of my sorrow. Matthew was dedicated to God as a baby. Throughout childhood he was taught the fundamentals of salvation at both home and church. When he was sick, he would ask for prayer. His belief in God and answered prayer, plus encouragement from the Bible, provides a strong hope for his salvation.

Rev. Ralph Shelton presiding over Matthew's dedication in 1982

When death strikes and questions arise that require answers one doesn't have, it's best not to dwell on those uncertainties. Embrace the positive memories, and leave the rest in God's hands. If the deceased's spirituality is in question, it's also sensible to leave that resolution in God's hands. Try to remember positive moments, and don't concern yourself with the unknown. Just remember the best of times while moving forward through the grieving process. It helps to retain all unsurpassed reminiscences deep within the heart.

One special memory shared by Matthew's aunt was when she saw him in church when he stood, head bowed and eyes closed, just days before his death.

"For if their rejection is their reconciliation of the world, what will their acceptance be but life from the dead" (Romans 11:15)?

"Believe in the Lord Jesus, and you will be saved—you and your household" (Acts 16:31).

Everywhere I'm looking for him, in the faces of young men in places he would go. Will I see him at a music store, strumming a model guitar? Or will I glimpse him as he boards a crowded elevator? Could he be the lead guitarist in his own band?

I THINK OF HIM

When winter blows
in drifts of snow,
I think of him,
his eyes aglow.

And all the young girls
that I meet
he could be kissing
in the street.

He would have grown
to six feet tall.
With friends he'd loafer
at the mall.

He'd be a star
in his own band,
a favorite guitar
in his hand.

Oh, how I yearn
to hear him say,
"I love you, Mom.
I'm back to stay."

©*Phoebe Leggett*

"There is no fear in love. But perfect love drives out fear, because fear has to do with punishment. The one who fears is not made perfect in love" (John 4:18).

Perhaps it's difficult to revisit places that allow memories of the past to surface regarding your loved one. It may be best to protect yourself, for a time, from this distress. Choose not to visit those places until you're ready to confront and lay aside your emotions of sorrow. Grief has no guidelines to surrender to. Feelings of sadness will come and go at will without boundaries to thwart the inevitable.

CHAPTER FOUR

How to Grieve

It's imperative that a proper amount of time be laid aside for grieving, and that you give yourself permission to lament. Mourning brings healing and resolution. Your dark tunnel of sorrow may be long in duration, but God can restore with joy and give you peace. "Weeping may endure for a night but joy comes in the morning" (Psalm 30:5 KJV).

A person who is grieving cannot function at one-hundred-percent capacity the initial days and months following the death of a loved one. Patience and understanding is needed during this period of time. Accept assistance when offered, and allow yourself time to recover from the trauma of loss. It's your time to grieve. Use this time wisely in order to transition through sorrow during this stage of grief.

It's also important to refrain from making key decisions at this time. If possible, wait at least one year following the death of a loved one, as issues associated with grieving could cloud good judgment.

"Now is your time of grief, but I will see you again and you will rejoice, and no one will take away your joy" (John 16:22).

"I tell you the truth, you will weep and mourn . . . You will grieve, but your grief will turn to joy" (John 16:20).

"The month when their sorrow was turned into joy and their mourning into a day of celebration" (Esther 9:22).

I AM NOT WHOLE

I am not whole.
I feel so weak.
I'm grieving for
life incomplete.

A hurt so deep
to feel such shame
at all the struggle
without the gain.

Mistakes were made.
It's hard to atone
a weight that's borne
on me alone.

My life feels spent.
I tried so hard
to fill the gap
but it's been marred.

I was waiting for
new change ahead,
but your death caused
deep sorrow instead.

©Phoebe Leggett

There's never a wrong, or a right way to mourn. Lamenting may be private or collective. Grieving can be loud or hushed. At times, wrenching sobs will leave you gasping for air. Charring emotions can smolder into the very depths of your soul and leave nothing but ashes and ruin. Writhing sensations may charge in and greet you before you're fully awake in the morning.

Unprocessed emotions will tug at your insides until it feels you're going to burst. Tears can gush forth at any given time. Out-of-control torrents may spill from your eyes in blinding downpours of sorrow. Unexpected outbursts of emotion will make you crazy. Unrestrained sentiment can send you into a spin and leave you reeling. Raw, open wounds are easy to penetrate and may deplete your very strength in a short amount of time.

Bible History on Grieving

The Israelites knew how to grieve. They would wear sackcloth on the body and ashes on the head while mourning a death, or grieving a sinful choice they had made. Sackcloth and ashes was the garment of mourning, and a witness to others that grieving was underway and in full process. The mourners would walk the street wearing sackcloth and ashes, or sit among the residue outside the gate of the city. This ritual would last for thirty days, the designated time of sorrow. During this period they could wallow in their sorrow. After the rite was completed, the grievers cleansed themselves, left their anguish behind, and continued to live their lives.

Although the rituals of mourning in today's society are quite different from the era of Bible days, the internal hurt remains the same. Examples given in the Bible on how to mourn represent an overall way to grieve. The Word of God gives us permission to lament. Many examples of being sorrowful are found throughout the pages of the Bible, and give a historical account of the grieving process. The Israelites, our best exemplar, had many reasons to grieve. They were the experts.

After the initial shock of losing a loved one has subsided, and a selected amount of time has passed, try to pick up the pieces of your life, and begin to exist again. When we allow God to heal our hurts, His remedy will complete the process.

The Bible on How to Grieve

"When Mordecai learned of all that had been done, he tore his clothes, put on **sackcloth** and **ashes**, and went out into the city, wailing loudly and bitterly" (Esther 4:1).

"O my people, put on **sackcloth** and roll in **ashes**; mourn with bitter wailing as for an only son, for suddenly the destroyer will come upon us" (Jeremiah 6:26).

"Then Jacob tore his clothes, put on **sackcloth** and mourned for his son many days. All his sons and daughters came to comfort him, but he refused to be comforted. 'No,' he said, 'in mourning will I go down to the grave to my son.' So his father wept for him" (Genesis 37:34).

"Then David said to Joab and all the people with him, 'Tear your clothes and put on **sackcloth** and walk in mourning in front of Abner.' King David himself walked behind the bier. They buried Abner in Hebron, and the king wept aloud at Abner's tomb. All the people wept also" (2 Samuel 3:31).

"In the streets they wear **sackcloth**; on the roofs and in the public squares they all wail, prostrate with weeping" (Isaiah 15:3).

"So put on **sackcloth**, lament and wail . . . " (Jeremiah 4:8)

"The elders of the Daughter of Zion sit on the ground in silence; they have sprinkled **dust** on their heads and put on **sackcloth**. The young women of Jerusalem have bowed their heads to the ground. My eyes fail from weeping, I am in torment within, my heart is poured out on the ground . . . " (Lamentations 2:10, 11)

"They will shave their heads because of you and will put on **sackcloth**. They will weep over you with anguish of soul and with bitter mourning" (Ezekiel 27:31).

"I will turn your religious feasts into mourning and all your singing into weeping. I will make all of you wear **sackcloth** and shave your heads. I will make that time like mourning for an only son and the end of it like a bitter day" (Amos 8:10).

A SEASON OF MY LIFE

July twenty-eight my youngest son
in a car crash lost his life
at the tender age of twenty-two.
This stabbed my heart like a knife.

What will I do? What will I say?
How will I react on a normal day?
Will the pain recede and loose its grip,
or will it never go away?

My heart-it aches. It hurts so bad.
The pain is so severe.
My eyes, so red—the tears won't stop.
My mind, so full and will not clear.

Although I know God's in control
as I lay down for the night,
in my heart, I'll always know
things will never be quite right.

Quiet moments may bring some relief as memories of good times resurface. But following those memories is the reality of death as the truth of it closes in around you. Those nearby may not notice when you're grieving because you're brokenhearted in silence. A song may trigger a session of tears and sorrow. An event or holiday may recapture the fun times, but the dreadful truth of why things aren't quite right will wrap around your mind. In an instant, you're back in the dreaded cycle of grief again. This sequence of mourning has now become your reality.

DID YOU KNOW?

Did you know
and that they say
your heart can break
and fall away?

Your heart can fracture,
be crushed and split?
It can be damaged;
no longer be fit.

My heart's been broken
by a life that is hard.
My son is now dead;
my heart now a shard.

My soul is in pieces,
and shattered, it seems.
Since my son's cruel death,
old hopes are just dreams.

This truth has now come.
My heart is not well.
It's fractured and crushed,
yet others can't tell.

©Phoebe Leggett

Listed below are suggestions that should help minimize the hurt of sorrow during the stages of grieving.

- Talk about your loved one on a regular basis. Mention them by name, and in conversation each day.
- If you're sad, say so. Don't try to hide your feelings.
- If you need extra help, don't be afraid to ask.
- Journaling is a great way to express your feelings.

- Continue positive routines each day. Be sure to exercise and eat right to maintain your own health and well-being.
- Join a grief-recovery or grief-support group.
- Continue to pray for God's comfort and help. Don't be afraid to ask others to pray for you.

Grieving God's Way, a book written by Margaret Brownley, indicates it may take as long as five years to work through the heartache of losing a loved one. For others, it will be longer. Don't try to rush the grieving process. Only time can heal a broken heart. And, only God can repair a damaged soul.

BROKEN HEART

I just miss you
oh, so much.
Life keeps moving
in such a rush.

People passing by
but they don't know
my heart is broken
and healing slow.

©*Phoebe Leggett*

CHAPTER FIVE

Emotions of Fear

Fear is an emotion that often emerges following the death of a loved one. You may be terrified that you'll be the next one to die. Or you may be afraid someone else close to you will pass away in the immediate future. Panic and dread can be devastating if allowed to overtake the mind. Apprehension of the future can be upsetting if permitted to continue. Nightmares, terror, and phobias may also surface. However, it's important to understand that fear is a normal reaction following the death of a loved one and shouldn't linger for long.

NEVER AGAIN

You will always be twenty-two.
You will never be old or new.
You will never again call and say,
"Mom, I'm home" again today.

Never again will you laugh or smile.
Never again will you stay a while.
Never again will you give a hug.
Never again will you show your love.

No more birthdays will come and go.
Life will never be fast or slow.
You will never again stay the night.
All is dark, and gone is the light.

No gifts to give with your name on them.
No mail, or cards, or letters from friends.
No one will call to talk to you.
No bride to you will say 'I do.'

There won't be children with your name.
You'll never achieve wealth or fame.
Holidays without you will have no meaning;
Memories about you only come by dreaming.

No more vacations with you in mind.
No more learning of any kind.
No more driving that sporty car.
No more traveling from near to far.

Your life is over. Your dreams are dead.
All hopes for you are crushed instead.
Life without you won't be the same;
and always tears when we mention your name.

But I'm so glad I shared your life
For all it was—there still was strife.
Though short is was, it still was yours;
and for the hurt you left—no cures.

"Whether a tree falls to the south or to the north, in the place where it falls, there will it lie" (Ecclesiastes 11:3).

After death nothing can be altered, or changed. It is what it is. Although difficult to accept, it's best to alleviate some of the sorrow when possible. One way is to focus on your loved one's accomplishments. Appreciate the relationship you shared, and recall memories that bring laughter and pleasure. Reclaim those moments, and cherish them as personal treasure.

A youthful death takes away part of the family legacy for all future generations. Children that would have been born will never exist. A potential son-in-law or daughter-in-law will never enhance the holiday gatherings. The family tree won't flourish with volumes of branches and bouquets of leaves. Instead, some of the limbs will remain empty and barren. Life will be hollow without the joy and excitement of a full house. What was normal and routine has now become irregular and unusual. All that's left are memories of the past, and sorrow for what could have been.

REMEMBER THE GOOD TIMES

We don't always
have to be sad.
Just remember the good times
that he had.

Remember his birthdays,
and his birth.
Remember the wonder,
and count the worth.

Remember the swing
in the backyard.
Remember ballgames
when he played hard.

Remember his laughter,
the fun that he had.
Remember his jokes
when we were sad.

Remember excitement
when Christmastime came;
his surprise and delight
with that new-fangled game.

Remember vacation
with sand, crabs, and ocean.
His cool guitar playing,
notes strung with emotion.

We don't always
have to be sad.
Remember the good times
that he had.

The best memories of my deceased son are the funny happenings that occurred during his childhood. Although the innocence of youth passed too soon, many humorous events continue to bring joy and laughter. Those moments are delightful to recall, and help to ease personal pain and sorrow.

Recalling Childhood Antics

Matthew would make the cutest remarks that were, in reality, quite profound. One remains a favorite.

While watching a thunderstorm approach, two-year-old Matt, deep in childish wonder, piped up, and said, "The thunder claps its hands. The bad clouds pushed the good clouds away."

When he was an active ten-year-old, our family spent the weekend camping in the Blue Ridge Mountains of western North Carolina. He loved playing hard, and his clothing was always covered in dirt and mud. One evening he was sent to the bathhouse for a shower, and reminded to wash away the debris he was covered in. But, predictable Matt had forgotten his towel.

Another camper was waiting outside the bathhouse for his turn in the shower when a clean Matthew emerged. When asked if the camper saw him naked, he said, "Oh, no. I had the shampoo bottle between my legs."

Grief Recovery

Your loved one's death may have been unexpected as caused by an accident, or sudden illness. Perhaps their demise was anticipated. Whether expected or not, the startling shock of that event will reverberate into your psyche.

It's important to have someone to talk with that understands your sorrow. The best assistance for grief recovery is to share your pain with others. Family and friends will be your best resource. You don't have to travel this road alone. And don't be afraid to ask for help from clergy or a medical professional. Take advantage of this time to recover with tools that will benefit you for the rest of your life. It could be an investment that saves your sanity.

Resist the urge to lock yourself away and grieve alone. The world is full of grieving people. Sharing your distress with others can help reduce feelings of sadness. In return, their support will convey comfort through words of encouragement. There will always be someone who cares.

Churches and various organizations offer resources and assistance to those who are grieving the loss of a loved one. The Internet provides an abundance of free information that will enable interaction with others. And many other outlets are available that encourage discussions and forums on how to grieve. Books and pamphlets on grief recovery are available at bookstores, funeral chapels, libraries, and churches. It's encouraging to realize that others are willing to offer assistance while on your journey through grief.

I MISS HIM EVERY DAY

I miss him every single day.
I miss him every kind of way
that pieces of my heart will break.
Sometimes it's more than I can take.

I miss him when the cars I see
remind me of his driving spree.
I miss him when he would rush in
leaving doors to slam right behind him

I miss his silly kind of grin
when I was looking right at him.
I miss him for his memory string
for he remembered everything.

I miss him when the sad songs play.
I wish this hurt would go away.
I miss him calling, "Hello . . . Hello,"
sometimes fast, and sometimes slow.

I miss him when the family meets
for he's not here. It makes me weep.
I miss his style of clothes and hair.
I miss his silly underwear.

But now that he has gone away,
I miss him more than I can say.

©Phoebe Leggett

"For I am the Lord, your God, who takes hold of your right hand and says to you, 'Do not fear; I will help you.'" (Isaiah 41:13).

"So do not fear, for I am with you; do not be dismayed, for I am your God. I will strengthen you and help you; I will uphold you with my righteous right hand" (Isaiah 41:10).

"Be strong and courageous. Do not be afraid or terrified . . . for the Lord your God goes with you; he will never leave you nor forsake you" (Deuteronomy 31:6).

JUST BE MY FRIEND

Just grieve with me,
and understand
the pain in my heart.
Just be my friend.

Just cry with me,
and hold my hand,
and feel my hurt.
Just be my friend.

Just be with me
and help me mend.
And let me talk.
Just be my friend.

Just pray with me
'till I can stand.
Just be with me.
Just be my friend.

©Phoebe Leggett

CHAPTER SIX

Emotions of Anger

Anger, a very real emotion, often surfaces following the death of a loved one. You may not be an angry person by nature, but grief is a strong sensation that can emerge in unbelievable ways. Pondering the recent death of a loved one may bring resentment, or some measure of rage. You may be annoyed at the one who has died. Or, you can be enraged at the situation that caused the death. Slight irritation, or an abundance of wrath, may surface when least expected. Some have even been angry at God, blaming him for their loved one's death.

WHEN YOU DIED

When you were happy,
a part of me cheered.
When you were scared,
a part of me feared.

When you were hurt,
a part of me felt pain.
When you were ignored,
a part of me felt shame.

When you were alone,
then I too felt alone.

And when you were angry,
a part of me was stone.

When you were hungry,
A part of me felt empty.
And when you were dressed up,
a part of me felt lovely.

When you were honored,
a part of me felt pride.
And when you were unhappy,
a part of me then cried.

But when you died,
more than a part of me died.

©Phoebe Leggett

Anger following the death of a loved one can overtake you in such an overwhelming way that it may damage your ability to remain balanced and coherent. Unexpected sensations will flood your mind and body as you try to rationalize the facts of your loved one's demise. Memories of the past may intermingle with the present, causing an inability to function in a rational way. Anxiety will be overwhelming as you struggle through your rage. Resentment and irritation can become your middle name.

Flossie and Freddie

Several years ago, I noticed a kitten stranded on the side of a busy street. It wasn't yet old enough to be on its own. Heavy trucks rolled down this road all day long. Somehow, the small kitten hadn't been killed. Its hungry cries of abandonment caught my attention, and I crossed the road to rescue it.

Since I was traveling, Flossie became my adopted companion. When we returned home she joined our growing feline family, and became the soul mate of Freddie, Matthew's kitten.

The feline bonding of the kittens was instantaneous, and soon they were inseparable. Both would snuggle in a shared basket under the window. They ate food at the same time, and shared all the toys. As constant companions, their bond was a reminder of their love for each other. If one disappeared for a short time, the other would cry out until they were reunited. This relationship was unique and special—a love match made in feline heaven.

One year later, Flossie disappeared. A distraught Freddie positioned himself by the door in watchful anticipation of her return, his soulful eyes gazing with sadness into the distance. He longed for her, and every action reflected his feelings. His soul mate was gone, and he was confused. His grief became obvious as feelings of sorrow consumed him. He moped about, looking dejected and forlorn.

Missing posters yielded no result and, over time, Freddie realized Flossie wasn't coming home. He became reclusive and unresponsive. His appetite diminished as he continued to grieve for her. After several weeks of patient waiting, he stopped his surveillance at the door. And, he never again bonded with another cat, but became a loner.

This was heart-wrenching and difficult to watch; a sad ending to a wonderful attraction. Freddie's demeanor was forever changed. My heart ached for him. And I grieved over Flossie, missing her as much as Freddie loved her.

Freddie was angry that Flossie was gone. But I was more enraged that my son was dead. In both our hearts, there was a lack of understanding.

Did I have a right to be angry with God? No. It would be wrong to blame God. My anger has been placed in the laps of those who deserve it.

My Anger

In 1981, when I told my then husband, a church pastor, that our third baby was on the way, he exploded. "Get an abortion!" he shouted. "If you don't, I'll tell everyone this baby isn't mine!" By his words he placed a spiritual curse on our unborn child, thus abandoning him even before his birth. How could he?

But I was going to have this child. I wanted this baby. And, because abortion is murder, it was never an option.

Over time it was obvious that Matthew had inherited his father's good looks, and charismatic personality. He was, without a doubt, his father's son. But his dad was an abusive man who detested married life. Because he hadn't enjoyed parenting his first two children, he certainly wasn't happy about our new addition. It was a difficult time in family history. We were divorced when Matthew was three.

Matt, as a teen, struggled for identity. His father could have given him a sense of self, but didn't. Birthdays and Christmases passed with the regularity of time, but without recognition from his father. In 1999, my ex-husband, the father of my children, passed away from cancer.

As a young adult, Matthew needed serious reinforcement, and a different direction. A plea for involvement from relatives on his father's side was declined as their lifestyle refused space for a misguided youth. Only after he became homeless did they offer assistance. But timing was crucial and intervention somewhat late. A lack of concern from Matthew's birth father, and others, made this road difficult to travel.

Would I be angry at God because he took my son? Did I love my son more than I loved Him? Although I chose not to blame God, many do. Anger is crucial to the grieving process. It helps to process this stage of sorrow by venting emotions of rage and resentment. However, those oppositions need to be expressed in appropriate ways so others aren't harmed in the process.

KICKING AND SCREAMING

Kicking and screaming
that's what I want to do.
To say over and over,
I know this isn't true.

Is this reality?
Who's at fault anyway?
Why did all this happen?
Just make it go away.

Will I ever feel better?
Will I ever calm down?
I really don't think so.
My child is in the ground.

©Phoebe Leggett

Sin and Death

Its best not to accuse God for the death of a loved one but to understand what ignited this derivation. Satan is the instigator of all deception. Because of his trickery, Adam and Eve sinned. And, because of their sin, disease and death were introduced into the world.

"Then the Lord God said to the woman, 'What is this you have done?' The woman said, 'The serpent deceived me, and I ate'" (Genesis 3:13).

"Therefore, just as **sin** entered the world through one man, and **death** through **sin**, in this way **death** came to all men . . . " (Romans 5:12)

"Nevertheless, **death** reigned from the time of Adam to the time of Moses, even over those who did not **sin** by breaking a command, as did Adam, who was a pattern of the one to come" (Romans 5:14).

SILENT CRIES

It's hard to see through tears
that veil large, swollen eyes
as anger, pain, and hurt
give way to silent cries.

©*Phoebe Leggett*

You may be annoyed at the timing of a loved one's death. Perhaps reconciliation didn't have a chance to take place. Anger could be aimed at someone else without realizing the reason for your outrage. Resentment may be overwhelming because of the way a loved one died. For the good of yourself and others, it's best to let the rage go. Try working through your anger issues without blaming others. Internalized resentments can paralyze emotions, and thus hinder the grieving process. Allow the Word of God to be your guide as you transition from anger into forgiveness.

CHAPTER SEVEN

Emotions of Regret

If a loved one struggled with disease and pain, there may be relief at their passing. It doesn't accomplish anything to experience regret over those feelings. Try putting your thoughts into perspective, and realize your loved one is no longer suffering. If a Christian when they died, their desired goal has been realized. Allow that comfort to sustain you while working through your sorrow.

Personal Regret

It's been difficult filtering beyond the personal guilt I've experienced following the death of my son. The "what ifs," questions of regret, are hard to overcome. But if I'm prepared to spread the guilt around, I should also be first in line to claim my rightful place. For, without a doubt, I carry a huge load of responsibility on my own head, justified or not.

I should have been more sensitive to my son's desires. I should have been more accessible, more accommodating, and more supportive of his personal dreams and wishes. And, I should have been more affectionate even though I was experiencing my own set of difficulties during our last year under the same roof.

Matthew—a self-portrait

Following Matthew's graduation from high school, my husband Dana's employer moved our family from Texas to Tennessee. Because Matt wasn't prepared to live on his own, he had to move with us. His rebellion surfaced shortly before the move, and continued for several years. After the transfer, he began attending college but failed all his courses, and was expelled. He then found a job and became friends with coworkers and their associates. But these friendships led him to drink alcohol and use drugs. A couple had criminal records. Over time, Matt himself had several brushes with the law. He wrecked his car and every car he owned thereafter. And, after three years of serious revolts, he ended up living on the street.

Although raised in a Christian household, Matthew's training seemed to have little impact on his behavior. But that doesn't lessen my own guilt. Had I realized the impact of his choices, I would have chosen another course to follow. However, retrospect comes too late to make a difference. And, if I been more aware of his medical condition, I would have realized that AS was a primary contributor to the destructive choices he was making. Better decisions on my part could have produced a more positive outcome.

At times guilt has overtaken my senses as I've tried to rationalize everything I've felt responsible for in my son's life. Serious thoughts of regret often surface. But since there's nothing I can do to alter the past, my only recourse is to forgive myself, and try to move on with my life.

I REMEMBER

Love is strong
when hearts are tender.
I think of you
and I remember

your childhood years.
I remember them all.
The things you did
when you were small.

You loved it all;
and as you grew,
everything to you
was fresh and new.

The excitement of life
with friendships rich and good;
laughter your middle name,
and laugh you always would.

And then you grew to man
while making choices wrong;
your life became a burden,
that crushed your happy song.

You lost all you had gained,
and had to start anew;
but I was nowhere near
to show my love to you.

Yet I remember you,
my young adventurous one.
Your life was not in vain;
you are my precious son.

©Phoebe Leggett

Learn from your mistakes, accept what cannot be changed, pardon yourself, and release all regret.

A Spark of Personality

Matthew had a unique way of speaking whatever came to mind. His granny recalled how adult he articulated his words, even as a three-year-old. Matt, toys in hand, spent a quiet morning with her while she visited with a friend. As he played by himself in the room, Granny and her friend chatted nearby. All of a sudden, Matthew stopped his play, looked his granny squarely in the face, and asked, "Now, what was that you just said?" Granny and her friend were astounded at his interest, as they had no idea he was listening to their conversation.

His other grandmother remembered an incident while shopping with four-year-old Matthew at the grocery store. A rather heavyset lady carrying an oversized handbag ambled past their shopping cart, and stopped in the bread aisle nearby. Matt stared at her, hand on chin, and then asked, "Do you think your pocketbook's big enough?"

Every spring, Matthew and his two siblings, Dawn and Brian, played little league baseball. Once the players were assigned a team, the new coach called each member to discuss the practice schedule with them.

One evening the telephone rang, and Matthew skipped over to answer it. His brother's coach was calling. After saying "hello", a strange look crossed his face. He then asked the caller, "What kind of house are you?" and handed the phone to Brian.

Brian looked puzzled. "Who is it?"

"It's your baseball coach, Mr. House," Matthew said. But under his breath he mumbled, "What kind of name is *House*?"

Memories are all that's left once a loved one has passed. At this point, feelings of remorse need to be laid to rest. Take time to concentrate on happier moments spent with your loved one, and put aside depressive thoughts and emotions.

CHAPTER EIGHT

Pit of Despair

Harboring feelings of rage, sorrow, disbelief, regret, and blame are often difficult to overcome. Twisted thoughts, angry spurts, and the desire to condemn others are all normal reactions following the death of a loved one. However, at some point, those negative emotions must be relinquished, and put into proper perspective.

Appreciate positive memories, refute negative ones, and move ahead with a determination to survive your sorrow. Refrain from placing blame, even on yourself. Remember your loved one for who they were, and allow an optimistic outlook into your future to surface. If one harbors regret, and finds it difficult to forgive, relinquish all that hurt to God whose unending love and mercy will saturate your soul. Leave the pain in the hands of the One who's more than able to embrace the anguish, and give you peace.

"That is why I am suffering as I am. Yet I am not ashamed, because I know in whom I have believed, and am convinced that **he is able** to guard what I have entrusted to him for that day" (2 Timothy 1:12).

"Now may the Lord of **peace** himself **give you peace** at all times and in every way" (2 Thessalonians 3:16).

ALL THAT'S LEFT

All that's left
are broken hearts,
shattered dreams,
unfinished starts.

All that's left
are ashes in an urn,
buried next a granite marker,
covered by a funeral fern.

All that's left
are lonely visits,
holiday sadness
with graveyard limits.

All that's left,
as life goes on,
is daily withdrawal
and being alone.

All that's left
is missing you
day and night,
in shades of blue.

All that's left,
when life is through,
is looking forward
to being with you.

Following an unexpected death are feelings of horrific despair. The sudden realization that you're not in control, and are powerless to go backward, may cause depressive thoughts and desperate actions. Still, it's best to mourn in your own way as you shuffle through the grieving process. Don't be afraid to express your feelings, as they may generate some closure to your misery.

In the Pits

As soon as I heard the news of my son's death, my mind began to scramble. I had a funeral to plan. This should never happen to a parent. I was very aware of my inexperience at making committal arrangements. The hospital needed to know where to send my son's body. *What are they saying? I'm not ready to bury my child.* But I'm grateful for sensitive funeral directors who were accommodating and supportive while walking us through the process of preparation and burial.

Subsequent to the death of my son, I acquired all information available regarding his accident. I needed to know the truth for myself. Medical reports from ambulance technicians, emergency room doctors and nurses, and other relevant information regarding Matt's short stay in the hospital were requested. Written reports from police officers at the scene, as well as verbal information, were received. Although strenuous, oral communication was part of the process. But the most difficult to grasp was a medical report in graphic form illustrating Matthew's heartbeats until the very last one. A straight line on the heart monitor printout was the hardest to ingest. This report demonstrated Matt's recorded first heartbeats as strong, but within just minutes the throbs began to decrease until the final beat.

"Thy dead men shall live, together with my dead body shall they arise. Awake and sing, ye that dwell in dust: for thy dew is as the dew of herbs, and the earth shall cast out the dead" (Isaiah 26:19).

The cardiologist's report inspired this poem which indicates a heartbeat's rhythm until it stops beating forever.

GONE

Gone
before the cloud could mist
Gone
before the flick of a wrist

Gone
before the minute hand moved

Gone
before your worth had been proved

Gone
after your last breath was drawn
Gone
before the birds have all flown

Gone
leaving others standing 'round
Gone
before hearing the next sound

Gone
after your last heart beat
Gone
no more words left to speak

Gone
no more time to give
Gone
no more life to live.

Gone
in the blink of an eye
Gone
nothing left but to die.

©*Phoebe Leggett*

Grieving may be a new experience for you. Try not to torture yourself as you consolidate your feelings. Realize your actions will have an impact on those around you. If you feel out of control, find someone to talk to. It may help to write your thoughts and feelings in a journal. Putting words on paper could be the best way to express your grief. It's also important to verbalize, and not internalize, your sorrow.

DON'T WANT TO KNOW

No . . . no . . . no . . . no.
It isn't so.
Please don't tell me;
don't want to know.

He is not dead.
He's just not dead.
He just went to
his room instead.

"Going to work.
I'm in the zone,"
I hear him call.
"I'm on the phone.

I'll be ready;
minute or two.
Give me a sec
I'm almost through."

Please don't tell me
don't want to know.
My heart beats fast,
my movements slow.

Then it comes back
in awful rush.
He is not here.
I feel a crush.

He truly died
—left me alone.
And he is not
just on the phone.

He's not inside.
He is no where.
My mind tells me
it's just not fair.

Yet all my heart
will not believe
that he's not here;
he didn't leave.

He's really just
in the next room.
My memories say
I'll see him soon.

©Phoebe Leggett

Sharing the Pain

A young lady called a few days after Matthew's burial. Her desire was to share her innermost feelings with the mother of the one she loved.

From her I learned that she and Matt had been in love. Their relationship had been ongoing, albeit from a distance, as they lived in separate states. Her call ignited many tears as she revealed her heart's cry. Our conversation lingered well into the night as we grieved together.

Several years have passed since Matthew death, and yet her love for him continues. Her emotional expressions stream forth in heartbreaking dialogue on the pages of an online condolence booklet provided by the funeral home for grieving family and friends. It's heartrending, yet sweet and personal. It's a love note from her to him that remains for all to read.

To Matt's mom: I'm sorry for the wonderful son you lost. If you knew him as well as I did, you would know that we loved each other very much. I think too much, but too late. I was supposed to be his perfect wife and him my perfect husband. He would always say he wanted a boy named Jose and a girl named Maria. But I left him. I'm so sorry, so sorry. Just know that I loved him so much. If I knew that was going to be the last time I was going to see him, I would have ran away with him. But I was so young. I'm sorry for your loss.

~

From a friend of hers: Two nights ago, I was in the deepest sleep ever in my life. My cell phone went off at 3:00 a.m. It was my best friend. She was crying so much it scared me. Then she told me the unfortunate news. I said out loud "Matt, this is a bad joke." But it wasn't. I was glad when she came back to Dallas. In my heart, I was wishing I would be a bridesmaid at their wedding. I remember the first and last time I saw him. He was so nice. I couldn't believe it has almost been a year since this horrible accident happened. I pray for his family, and most of all that his soul is happy with the Lord. Goodbye, Matt.

~

Tonight is one of those nights. You are on my mind. Matt, like a few years ago, I had my cell phone under my pillow so that when you called me no one would hear my cell ring. But you didn't call. And you won't. Te extrados mucho.

I have yet to figure out how to smile without you by my side. I don't know how to go on knowing what my life should have been. I talk to you every night until I fall asleep. I dreamed of you, and it made me believe that you are still here. Then I woke up and realized you really are gone, and I'm going to have to wait to see you again. I remember the first time you saw me. I was the most precious thing in this world to you. I remember the first time we kissed. We knew it was love. When will my pain leave? This is a question with a harsh reality. You will never leave my heart. No one will ever take your place. That is your home. And with that said, I will live with this pain. I love you. I miss you. And I love you!

Matt, I still don't get it. Why can't you be here with me? Another year has come and gone without you by my side. I feel so useless not being able to fill the emptiness you left in my life. We had so many plans. I tell myself I will have another chance. And I might, but how? I can't live our dreams with someone else, and I won't. I can't. I miss you so much. There is nothing in this world that could ever take the place of what you left in my heart. It hasn't changed. It never will. I loved you. I love you. And I will love you until my last breath, and after.

~

Tonight I wish I can fast forward to tomorrow so I don't have to deal with what I'm feeling right now. I feel the pain of loss—the dream life that should have been. I'm in a state of mind that I can't get out of, though. I feel I don't deserve to get out of it. I feel I don't deserve a happy life without you. I don't feel the need to have one either. My life was planned with you. I didn't think of a plan B; didn't think I'd need one. You promised, remember? It was going to work out . . . was.

I remembered the last time you and I ever spoke. I'm so sorry. I'm so sorry. I was always told to apologize when I do something wrong. But it really does no good. That doesn't change what happened—nor does it make it better. I've never seen the phrase so useless until now. I wish I could change things, Matt. I really wish I could. I miss you, Matt! I love you!

Remember the time we argued about why we were together? You called me from work, and I told you it was over. I felt with you so far away, what was the point? You begged me not to hang up, but I did. I wouldn't return your phone calls for two days. On the third day, I couldn't help but feel lost without your voice. It was around midnight when I decided to call. You answered really fast. It hit me! You knew I was going to call. You knew why we were trying to make things work. You knew we were perfect for each other. You told me everything I didn't know at the time. It didn't matter that I didn't know. You knew for us. I miss you so much!

When something hurts so much, I have to ask myself, what did I do wrong? I don't understand why things turned out so bad for us. In my heart, I thought we could overcome anything and everything. Why am I always wrong? I miss you! I need you!!

I miss you so much, and it's hard to believe another year has almost ended without you. I wish I could go back in time just to have one more day with you. I love you!

How am I surviving without you? It seems so unreal to think that I will not hear your voice again, not in this lifetime at least. Or at least I think until I fall into a deep sleep and see you there. That's the only time I'm truly happy. When I dream of you, everything seems to be right in my life. But at the end of every dream, I never get to say good-bye. When I dream, I forget it's not real. And in a second, my whole dream makes me realize how miserable my life truly is. I wish I could dream forever. I miss you! I love you!

I feel so sad knowing I will never have the opportunity to celebrate a Christmas with you. To never buy and wrap gifts together for our families or have a chance to put up a Christmas tree together. I don't understand what I did wrong to be deprived of such happiness. I miss you!

Merry Christmas—I love you, Matt, and I miss you.

Oh, how I wish I could bring in this year with you. I guess in a way I am. You are still, and always will be, in my heart. I miss you!

CHAPTER NINE

Holidays

Birthdays, anniversaries, and other holidays are difficult to celebrate following the death of a loved one. The toughest times of sorrow will be the ability to endure days of celebration. You may feel alone in your grief amid the fun and festivity of those around you. But you're not. Millions of people around the world are suffering the loss of a loved one. Grief is universal, and unites the inconsolable in one ache of anguish and sorrow.

Hiding emotions can become a secret addiction. It's best not to quench your feelings. Allow expressions of grief to occur. Include others who are also grieving, and give yourself time to process your sorrow. This is beneficial to emotional healing. The ability to remember joyful moments shared when your loved one was alive will help ease the burden of loss. Don't be afraid to grieve. Those moments can be therapeutic, and should improve over time. As expressed throughout the years, time is the only thing that can ease the load of grief. However, and in most cases, all sorrow doesn't completely go away. It only becomes easier to accept.

HOLIDAY SADNESS

In the middle of chaos,
in the middle of fun,
in the middle there is heartache,
because we're missing someone.

While everyone is busy,
and all are having fun,
surrounded by our loved ones,
still we're missing that someone.

It's always been great joy
when company has come.
With lots and lots to do,
Yet there's emptiness for some.

Almost everyone is here;
the little ones make it fun.
With lots of food and laughter,
I'm glad they all could come.

But I'm so sad
for the one
who couldn't come.

©Phoebe Leggett

After my son's death I didn't want to celebrate anything. The joy of commemorating the holidays was over. Tears would emerge at any unexpected moment, and sorrow was overwhelming when those special days stared me in the face. Christmas trees and colorful decorations no longer invited a joyful reunion. It was difficult to lay aside my sorrow in order to preserve the traditions of noteworthy holidays. My stash of Christmas treasures no longer brought happiness, and became useless clutter. Over time, most of my decorations were donated to the local thrift store. Only a few possessions remained as a memorial of past traditions and happier times. Holidays were just days to hurry through, try to endure, and then disengage from. The pain of loss was everywhere, and the struggle to find something worth celebrating was difficult. It was easier to curl up in a blanket and let the world go by.

At the beginning of each new year, my calendar is labeled with reminders of birthdays and special days. Even now, the tradition of marking the date of Matt's birth continues. Special days when he was alive remain a part of everyday living. He is, and always will be, an important member of our family. Samantha, my granddaughter and Matt's niece, takes great pleasure in watching videos of her Uncle Matt, her mother, and her Uncle Brian when they were small. She loves the connection. And, as she continues to grow, it's obvious that she and her Uncle Matt share several similar interests.

Samantha enjoys the notion of their similarities, and mentions her distress at not having her Uncle Matt around. Her consideration is soothing as she has great appreciation for someone she never had a chance to know. She is the catalyst for the continuation of family traditions as she includes everyone important to her, including the deceased members of her family.

Christmas Gift

By Cathy Pendola

Holidays, especially Christmas, are difficult. The first Christmas after losing Dominic, we put up a tree for my daughter's sake. But we were all choking back the tears. We lit a candle in front of Dom's picture as we opened our gifts. It all felt surreal. I wanted my old life back.

Christmas has always been my favorite holiday, and I felt like it was taken away from me. I think holidays, birthdays, and so on require me to do anything that gives me comfort. My son loved Starbucks. Each Christmas, I put out his stocking and put a gift card from Starbucks in it. Then I use the card when I go there to remember Dominic and how we would sometimes meet for coffee before school. I believe everyone, in their own way, finds a coping mechanism to deal with all the reminders of a loss. Slowly, you find your way.

Christmas Blur

By Belle Woods

Danny died the Wednesday after Thanksgiving in 2007. Christmas that year remains a blur. I just don't remember much about it except that some friends invited us over to their house, which was a comfort. Being in church and having fellowship with other believers has been one of the biggest supports and encouragements for me, especially during the holidays.

When Danny and I were first married, he was not a fan of Christmas. But I enjoyed Christmas very much. It took a couple of Christmases for Danny to realize it wasn't the way it had been for him as a child. He'd had many bad experiences and didn't want to see Christmas come that first year. But over time, he learned to love the holidays as much as I did. I miss him saying, "Merry Christmas, and remember, Jesus is the reason for the season!"

Don't be afraid to communicate your feelings to those around you. Your own words of sorrow could encourage others who are grieving a similar loss. New friendships have developed when sharing personal stories with people in comparable situations. Individuals grouped in related circumstances can be therapeutic. It's also important not to neglect yourself during this time of grief and restoration. Memories of happier times with your loved one can help to soften the blow of heartache.

Remembering the Good Times

Matthew could have been a stand-up comic. He had a unique ability of bringing laughter to the table. Even as an adult, his childlike delight for everything in his world energized those around him. Since laughter is the best medicine, he aimed to please. A hearty laugh was imminent at many unexpected moments. His invariable knack for being creative was amazing.

When Matt was eight years old, he designed a unique Christmas gift for Dana, his stepdad. His gift was presented in an oversized cardboard box covered in a colorful array of Scotch, masking, and duct tape. Inside the box was a designer monstrosity created from a combination of wood, nuts, bolts, cans, and many unnamed scraps of anything that could be attached. It didn't have a name or a function, but was just a large and useless conglomerate of cluttered junk. Needless to say, this construction brought bouts of laughter that exploded into the room. The hours that Matthew had spent designing this special gift were hard to ignore, and continues to bring unforgettable memories to mind.

LAUGHTER

He should have been called Isaac,
for he was full of fun.
From birth to twenty-two,
he was the laughing one.

His twinkling eyes were bright.
Concerns of life ignored.
He tried to make you laugh.
Your bliss was his reward.

Not once forgot a joke.
Memory brought them back in rhyme.
His satire was the best
of artists in his time.

©Phoebe Leggett

"A happy heart makes the face cheerful, but heartache crushes the spirit" (Proverbs 15:13).

"Even in laughter the heart may ache, and joy may end in grief"(Proverbs 14:13).

"Grieve, mourn and wail. Change your laughter to mourning and your joy to gloom" (James 4:9).

Birthdays, Thanksgiving, and Christmas can be the most difficult of times following the death of a loved one. The dining room table has an empty chair. Spontaneous chatter is no longer active. And the heaviness of sorrow is felt by all.

Samantha is missing the love and attention of an uncle she doesn't remember. Brian can no longer enjoy the bantering and camaraderie he shared with his brother, and he doesn't have a younger sibling to recall childhood memories with. Dawn doesn't have the brother she considered more like her in personality than any other family member. And, as parents, Dana and I no longer have our youngest to embrace, or lend a hand to.

But Matthew won't be a forgotten uncle, an absent sibling, or a missing family member. We will continue to talk about him as if he were present. The desire to engage in conversation with him, or discuss current events is a trial that must be dealt with even more when a holiday is observed. But memories of the past continue to merge with the present. This exchange allows for an ongoing connection between brother, uncle, mother, father, and child. In this way, our missing loved one can remain a part of the family circle. But in reality, a link will always be missing from family gatherings.

Oh, the Memories

Another precious memory surfaces whenever Christmas traditions involve the rituals of a visiting Santa Claus.

Christmas was a special time at our house. And, for Matthew, the excitement over Santa's visit was enormous. He would spend hours during the days before Christmas creating a trap to catch this elusive visitor. A maze of kite string was tied to door handles, closet knobs, bed posts, and every other piece of large furniture in his bedroom. This labyrinth of string would crisscross the room from wall to wall. Fragments of paper, small toys, and various sundry items were displayed as decoys throughout the snare.

Cookies and milk had their place on his bureau, available for his favorite visitor to enjoy. Matthew's plan was to ambush the caller, although his logic for doing so was never quite understood, or revealed.

Every year, Santa maneuvered through the trap to steal the edible treats. And he always left a note for the designer. Later on, when Matthew realized the truth of Santa's tricks, he remained impervious to that reality. Designing and constructing a new entrapping device became Matt's personal Christmas tradition, and continued for several delightful years.

TWO YEARS

Two sad years
have come and gone.
But you're not here.
It's been so long.

My heart—it aches
for you each day;
ever since
you went away.

©Phoebe Leggett

A Time for Everything

There is a time for everything, and a season
for every activity under heaven:
a time to be born and a time to die, a time to plant and a time to uproot,
a time to kill and a time to **heal**, a time to
tear down and a time to build,
a time to **weep** and a time to laugh, a time
to **mourn** and a time to dance,
a time to scatter stones and a time to gather them,
a time to embrace and a time to refrain, a time
to search and a time to give up,
a time to keep and a time to throw away, a
time to tear and a time to mend,
a time to be silent and a time to speak, a time to love and a time to hate,
a time for war and a time for peace (Ecclesiastes 3:1-8).

BIRTHDAY

Today was my son's birthday,
but he won't celebrate.
It's time for one more birthday,
but now it is too late.

All birthdays come and go.
but never quite the same.
The age of twenty-two
he always will remain.

CHAPTER TEN

When a Child Dies

"A voice is heard in Ramah, weeping and great mourning, Rachel weeping for her children and refusing to be comforted, because they are no more" (Matthew 2:18).

Losing a child in death can be the most devastating experience of a lifetime. Whether your child was stillborn, or lived to be ninety years old, he or she will always be of your flesh and blood. A part of you will die when your child does. Death is cruel, and the after-effects painful. Age has no bearing on this certainty. The emotional aspects of your loss can be catastrophic.

When a child you've waited for, cuddled, dressed, fed, and loved with every ounce of your being dies, it's enough to make a parent go insane. Although my child was twenty-two when he passed, he was still my baby. That reality will always be our bond.

"Remember not the sins of my youth and my rebellious ways; according to your love remember me, for you are good, oh Lord" (Psalm 25:7).

A PART OF ME

Close to my heart
but still in my womb,
I was there with you
until you were born.

Then I was there
to hold you long,
and kiss you gently
with lullaby song.

I was there for you
as you nursed my breast,
then lay your head
upon my chest

and slept your soft
gentle baby sleep.
As you dreamed I prayed
your soul to keep.

I was there for you
when you stumped your toe.
I watched you learn,
and watched you grow.

So thankful was I
but you couldn't yet see
that I'll love you always—
you are a part of me.

Then without warning you were killed.
How could I have known
your life would end this way,
and you would die alone?

Although it would be best to move on with your life following the death of a child, this blind, in-your-face reality makes that notion impossible. The term *time heals all wounds* will never fit parental bereavement. This relates to the death of a child far more than any other loss. The reverse connotation is more accurate, as more intense sorrow will surface as time goes on. Even more concentrated misery may occur in the third and forth years following the death of a child. To understand this truth is to accept the verity of death.

When a child is involved, there is no moving forward. Horror and grief are moments that will surround a parent for days, months, even years following the death of a child. For a prolonged period of time, it will be impossible to budge from this sorrow. Survival is accomplished only while anesthetized and numb every waking moment of every meaningless day. Anguish over the death of your own flesh-and-blood offspring can lead to mental de-fragmentation of all sanity. This torment is grueling and time-consuming, and may become even more painful as time goes on.

In *Mourning and Melancholia (1917),* Sigmund Freud makes a famous distinction between mourning, which is the normal reaction to the loss of a loved one, and melancholia, which is a form of mental illness. According to Freud, grieving people need to break free from the deceased, let go of the past, and begin again by going in a different direction. A healthy grief experience, according to Freud, is one in which the deaths of loved ones will not leave traces of any gross change in the bereaved. However, his concept has been proven false. Psychologists are now realizing the importance of maintaining bonds with the deceased, and demonstrate that a lifetime of grief is normal in cases of loss following the death of close friends and family members. This sorrow is even deeper when a child has died.

God's Comfort

The peace that passes all understanding, flowing from God above, was my only sanity during the days and months that followed the death of my son. I realized that God was in control even though I wasn't. His comfort continued to surround me like a blanket. Never before had I experienced such a calming presence. The Holy Spirit was there as promised in God's Word and hovered near, bringing peace and tranquility to my crushed and shattered soul.

"To comfort all who mourn" (Isaiah 61:2).

Satan tried to interject thoughts of hell into my mind to torture me. But when I said, "Satan, get behind me. Do *not* taunt me," the harassment stopped.

"And the peace of God, which transcends all understanding, will guard your hearts and your minds in Christ Jesus" (Philippians 4:7).

"Peace I leave with you; my **peace** I give you" (John 14:27).

"Who comforts us in all our troubles, so that we can **comfort** those in any trouble with the **comfort** we ourselves have received from God" (2 Corinthians 1:4).

Where is Assurance?

Do you need reassurance that you can survive your sorrow? Chapter twenty-three provides the complete plan of salvation.

"You will keep in perfect peace him whose mind is steadfast, because he trusts in you" (Isaiah 26:3).

"As a mother comforts her child, so will I comfort you; and you will be comforted" (Isaiah 66:13).

"I will turn their mourning into gladness; I will give them comfort and joy instead of sorrow" (Jeremiah 31:13).

GOD IS WITH ME

I know that God is with me.
I know He truly cares.
I know He'll never leave me.
I know He's always there.

I know for His Spirit
reminds me where I'm from;
assures me that I'm safe,
and that I'll overcome.

He brings me peace of mind
when my world falls apart.
He places joy within me,
and puts love in my heart.

When deepest sorrow comes
that takes my sleep at night,
I feel His Spirit with me.
He whispers, "It's alright."

©Phoebe Leggett

"Be merciful to me, O Lord, for I am in distress; my eyes grow weak with sorrow, my soul and my body with grief" (Psalm 31:9).

I've never understood why Matthew had to die so young. My prayer had always been that God would protect my children and cover them with His mercy. Because my prayers were faith based, I lived with the confidence that God's angels would hover near, and respond when needed. My belief was strong because God had answered many prayers for me.

Answered Prayer

Our family planned a trip from west Tennessee, where we lived, to North Carolina to visit family when Matt was seventeen. Since both boys wanted to drive their own cars, my husband and I conceded—with reservation. Neither had driven nonstop for seven hours before.

We began our trip as a convoy of three. During the trip, our cars became separated as more vehicles flooded the highway. Matthew was driving far ahead when traffic tightened near Nashville. Panic seized my mind, and fear overtook my senses. Brian was still in sight, but Matt had disappeared long before. At this point, I began to pray, and pray, and pray.

Dana exited the highway for a brief refueling. Standing at the gas pump was Matthew, grinning from ear to ear. Heart in throat, I poured out my thanksgiving to God for this incredible miracle. But that was just one of many answered prayers.

Was it still reasonable to be angry with God for Matt's death? The answer is still, "No."

JULY 28, 2008

To Matthew

Four years ago
this very day
you left this earth
and went away.

I see you run
without a care;
arms open wide,
a hug to share.

Your smile so clear,
with shy allure.
I miss you so.
There is no cure.

Mom

©Phoebe Leggett

Because God had honored my desire to have children, Matthew was born. Although his life ended after twenty-two years, God had kept him safe many times during his life. And now, without God's mercy, I had no desire to live—not for another day or another minute. I had to keep trusting in God. There was no one else.

It was natural for me to believe in God. I always had. Still, I was amazed that my sanity remained intact following the death of my son. But I was concerned for the rest of the family—my other children and my husband. How would they react to this tragedy? What were they feeling? How could I help them?

Dawn and her husband were scheduled to finalize the purchase of their new home the morning Matthew was killed. Following the news, their plans had to change. It was decided that Samantha would stay with her grandpa and me while they completed their acquisition. Also, the following day was Samantha's third birthday. Her celebration had already been scheduled.

Dawn and Samantha rushed to our home in Charlotte, arriving around nine o'clock that morning. The original plan was to drive to the funeral home as soon as they arrived. But our pastor had promised to be with us, so we decided to wait for his arrival. However, a few minutes past eleven, the church secretary called and informed us the pastor would not be coming.

Realizing precious minutes had been squandered, we rushed to the car and quickly drove to Ray's Funeral Home in Madison, North Carolina, about three hours away. We needed to see Matthew one last time, and make arrangements for his funeral.

Etched forever in infinity, this day will be the most horrible one ever lived. Each painful, excruciating moment was surreal. My child was dead, and trust in a cleric had been compromised.

Following our visit to the morgue, we drove to the home of my ex-husband's sister, the aunt of my children. Their home would be the designated receiving station for family and friends. An amazing abundance of prepared food from Matthew's employment, local churches, and friends of the family had been provided. Several flower arrangements had also been delivered. The dining room table revealed a huge spread of delicious cuisine for all to enjoy. I don't recall eating even one bite.

The following day, Dawn drove to Greenville, South Carolina, to meet her husband at the attorney's office to complete the purchase of their new home. What she remembers most, following the news of her brother's death, was driving many hours as she traveled between several states in order to complete her commitments.

Brian, the older son, had an important test to take at college that same day. He decided to remain at school as planned, as it would be difficult to reschedule his examination. The following morning, he and Michael, one of his friends, drove from Tennessee to our home in North Carolina. But their communication was minimal during the trip. Brian preferred not to speak, or to even think. He just wanted to get home and be with his family.

Details of that day remain blurred. But Dana, my husband, was a solid rock. He coordinated our plans as, together, we plunged headlong into our nightmare.

The Way It Is

"I felt very bad for the way Matthew died," Dana said. "I felt deep sorrow that he was so young. But he was gone, and I could do nothing for him. I felt sorry for you, his mother. I saw how painful this was for you. Matthew was your child, and the youngest one. He was your baby.

Timing was also a factor. When Matt died, your relationship with him was strained. My heart went out to you. I ached for you. After seven years of grieving, everyone else has moved on, but not you. No one will ever grieve over your son like you will. You are his mom. And because a mother's love runs deep, you'll never stop grieving for him. That's just the way it is."

But for God's Mercy

"He will never leave you nor forsake you" (Deuteronomy 31:8).

Why should I praise God now? My youngest was dead. Where was God's mercy when he died?

I admit there were times when I felt the answer to my prayers had been a bit slow in coming. But God had always been faithful. Every day, I would breathe a quick word of praise to Him. "Thank you for Your mercy," had long been my daily words of gratitude.

Over the years, God had answered many prayers for me. He'd made it clear that He was my help and strength. And the test of time had proven Him faithful. But what about this time? What about now?

It's true that God never promised to take my problems away. He only promised to be with me *through* them. Trust is what I had to do.

Following the crushing blow of my son's death, I tested God once more. "Thank you for Your mercy," I said in a faint whisper.

In an instant, there was God—bringing waves of comfort to surround me like a warm and fuzzy blanket. It was then I discovered that whatever happens in life, God would always be with me. His love and mercy would continue to surround me because I trusted in Him. And that's a promise I can live with.

"Thank you, God, for Your mercy that is new every morning. Amen."

For without God in the equation, there is no hope.

Bad News

When we received the news of my son's death, the family had yet to realize the magnitude of what was ahead. The news was implausible, mind-boggling, and difficult to grasp. We all operated in mechanical despondency while trying to comprehend the unbelievable. Those moments remain difficult to recall although more than seven years have passed since that terrible day.

But sharing those complicated times has allowed new friendships to develop with others who are grieving similar losses.

Losing My Son Dominic

By Cathy Pendola

I lost my wonderful son Dominic in a car accident in 2004. He was nineteen years old and had his whole life in front of him, or so I thought. I still can't believe he's gone. Losing a child changes the landscape of your life forever.

The first year after losing Dominic, I felt like I was walking around in a fog. I would get up each day and reality would hit me in the face the moment I opened my eyes. I did what I needed to do to get through the day. But some days I could barely take a shower. I wanted to stay in the house, be alone, and shut out the world. Weekends were especially hard because that was our time to be together as a family. But now a member of our family was missing. It was just my husband, daughter, and me sitting at a dinner table for four. We had to watch the waiter clear away the fourth place setting because no one would be joining us. Life goes on, but I felt as if I was standing still, watching.

Sometimes I wonder how my family and I have survived this tragedy. What I have learned is this is a day-to-day, one-foot-in-front-of-the-other process.

Reading has helped me. The books I can't get enough of are about near-death experiences and life after death. I know these are not books most people would want to read. But somehow they give me comfort. On some level, I'm searching for what this whole *after-life* thing is all about. I also know I'm looking for answers to a question that cannot be given in this life . . . why? Sometimes things happen that we have no control over and no explanation for.

It has been seven years now since I lost my son. And yes, time gives me perspective. I don't believe time heals all wounds—at least not this wound. What I've learned is to cherish everyone around you that you love. Tell them you love them and often. Appreciate all the moments you have together, and live in the moment. Life is wonderful, but fragile. We should handle it with care.

Our Little Missionary

By Carolyn K. Knefely

Little Miss Missionary
With death comes life.
With loss comes gain.
With Christ comes comfort
in bearing the pain.

©Carolyn K. Knefely

Breathing was a struggle for our newborn daughter, Carrie. Without a pallet or esophagus, taking nourishment between her tiny lips was impossible. So many other things went wrong because her body had given her one gene too many.

Leaning down, the doctor cleared his throat. "No heroics will change the outcome," he said. Carrie was given less than eight hours to live. He pronounced death, but Christ delivered life. Our little missionary lived eleven days.

Through Carrie's death, I found new life in walking closer to Jesus Christ. I hadn't read the Bible until dealing with her death and the lonely days that followed. Reaching daily for comfort in the Word of God, I gained new reasons to live. Now I celebrate Carrie's life even though it was short. I praise God for taking her because His little girl is now whole in His arms.

CHAPTER ELEVEN

When a Spouse Dies

Losing a spouse to death is the same as losing a part of you. What has been joined together has now been divided. This sorrow is a severe invasion into your life. Memories surround you from every direction. The common is now uncommon. What was normal is no longer normal. Your bed is empty, and your soul mate is missing. You realize the dining room table was built for more than one. Your helper is gone, and your entire pattern of life has changed. It's difficult to believe you're now alone.

Problems of forgetfulness may set in. In the past, you may have been organized. But after the death of your spouse, the focus has changed.

Disorganization and forgetfulness are normal following the death of a loved one. When appointments are missed, keys misplaced, and routine activities forgotten, poor memory and aggravation may become bothersome. Your struggle to conquer the sadness of losing your beloved will now consume your mind.

Try to be patient with yourself. Write notes as reminders of future scheduled appointments for reference when absentmindedness sets in. And don't be afraid to ask for help if you feel overwhelmed. Routine tasks may now take longer to complete than normal. An inability to manage time effectively can be difficult as projects remain unfinished.

Design your time wisely so important things are planned, thus making tasks easier to complete. Try focusing on new outlets that will help to ease your sense of loneliness. And don't become isolated from others, as interaction with friends and family is crucial for recovering from the emotions of sorrow. It's important to function well in order to continue living your life to the fullest.

A Widow's Reaction

As a woman, my mother was somewhat independent until my father passed away. A short time later she became edgy and fearful. Her phobia escalated until it was necessary to have an alarm system installed, complete with sensors and motion detectors. Even after installation she retained a serious lack of long-term trust in people. Routine household noises were cause for anxiety. Although she talked about her fears with everyone, she was unable to forget them. She lived in a safe environment, but that alone couldn't give her peace of mind.

My father had always kept my mother's car serviced with oil changes and tire checks. His diligence also maintained the property by mowing the lawn, raking leaves, and removing broken branches when necessary. And he kept the interior and exterior of the home repaired. The household was functional as long as my dad was alive.

However, following his death, several close neighbors had to provide assistance with the outdoor tasks my mother wasn't able to complete herself. And soon friends from the church became available when needed. An extended family of sisters, nieces, and nephews, always eager to help, were just a phone call away.

While issues of burial, finances, and loneliness are being resolved, painful memories may be difficult to surrender. Over time, those sad moments should be replaced with warm and happy thoughts as memories from the past come shining through. The heart will always hold a place for your beloved. But when it takes more time than expected to sort through those feelings, therapy or counseling with a cleric or professional counselor could be beneficial. It may be easier to accept help from a professional than a family member or close friend.

THE DEMAND

Who can rest
and who can sleep?
You had asked God
his soul to keep.

You trusted God
from where you sat.
The prayers were prayed,
and left at that.

Don't know just why;
can't understand.
You died but what
was the demand?

I needed you
and wanted you too.
Don't understand,
why rush you through?

Why, and what,
and when and where?
Questions asked;
it isn't fair.

It's just not fair
that you are dead;
your life now gone
and grief instead.

Your live is over.
It feels like mine.
And all that's left
are tears and time.

Time to remember,
time to reflect;
time to be sad,
time to regret.

I tried so hard
But now I'm numb
to make things better
but death had come.

There is no answer
to questions above,
but trust in this:
that God is love.

And whatever happened
was in God's plan.
To take you home
was the demand.

© *Phoebe Leggett*

Who will be my helpmate now? Can I survive all by myself? Who will assist me with the yard, or the house? Who will prepare my meals? Who will take care of my finances? Who can I depend on now? These questions, and more, will invade the mind and may cause some anxiety.

Now is the time to allow others to reach out to you. Don't shun their help, and don't be afraid to ask for it either. Accept the assistance of others, and let God to be a husband or wife to you. Only He can fill that void with His comfort.

WHO WILL?

When I'm feeling sad,
who will bring me cheer?
And when I'm all alone,
who is always near?

When I am crying
who will wipe my tears?
And when I am scared,
who will calm my fears?

When I am hurting,
who will feel my pain?
When I am senseless,
who makes me feel sane?

When I am hungry,
who will give me food?
And when I'm in despair,
who will calm my mood?

When I am in danger,
who will keep me safe?
And when I need a shelter,
who gives me a place?

When I am confused,
who will understand?
And when I am dying,
who will hold my hand?

Jesus knows and feels
everything I feel.
Jesus calms my fears,
for he is very real.

© *Phoebe Leggett*

"The **widow** who is really in need and left all alone puts her hope in God and continues night and day to pray and to ask God for help" (1 Timothy 5:5).

"Then you will call, and the Lord will answer; you will cry for help, and he will say: 'Here am I'" (Isaiah 58:9).

"Hear my prayer, O Lord, listen to my cry for help; be not deaf to my weeping" (Psalm 39:12).

"In my distress I called to the Lord; I cried to my God for help" (Psalm 18:6).

"But you, O Lord, be not far off; O my Strength, come quickly to help me" (Psalm 22:19).

"Yet I am poor and needy; may the Lord think of me. You are my help and my deliverer; O my God, do not delay" (Psalm 40:17).

"Surely God is my help; the Lord is the one who sustains me" (Psalm 54:4).

"Let us then approach the throne of grace with confidence, so that we may receive mercy and find grace to help us in our time of need" (Hebrews 4:16).

DUST

You were real
I could feel;
flesh and blood,
I could touch.
Now just dust.

Flesh to ashes
ashes to dirt;
too much hurt.
Metal to rust
it's just dust.

Lost in pain
Little gain
Only rain
Can't refrain
Who to blame?

No more trust
death a bust.
Ashes to ashes
dirt and rust.

Now you're gone.
You're just dust.

©Phoebe Leggett

"By the sweat of your brow you will eat your food until you return to the ground, since from it you were taken; for **dust** you are and to **dust** you will return" (Genesis 3:19).

Losing My Husband

By Belle Woods

When Danny died, I lost my best friend. We were friends before we became engaged and were inseparable. It has been over three years now, but it's still fresh. His death left a hole in my heart and in my life. During the night, I wake up thinking he's still asleep beside me, but I just find an empty pillow. Then the loneliness sets in. The only thing that helps is talking to the Lord. So I do until I fall back asleep.

I've had two gardening seasons since Danny passed away, but I'm not so sure about this year. The first year was very difficult. Danny wasn't an outdoor person, but he'd always helped me with the garden. In the evening, just before sunset, we'd go *walk together in the garden in the cool of the evening* to see how it was progressing. (Then the man and his wife heard the sound of the LORD God as he was walking in the garden in the cool of the day, (Genesis 3:8) Last summer, it was difficult for me to spend time in the garden. It was such a lonely place without him.

Going to Wal-Mart was difficult because the last eight years of Danny's life we were together 24/7, which meant we always went shopping together. Even after almost thirty years of marriage, I'd look up and see him come around the corner from an aisle and my heart would skip a few beats. I just loved him so much. Going shopping wasn't fun anymore. Three months after he died, a new Wal-Mart opened up. It's easier to shop there because the surroundings have changed.

My sleep had been insufficient several years before he died because I have fibromyalgia. But after he died, it became worse. I would go for nights without sleep, or I would cry myself to sleep. I asked my Aunt Eva, who had lost her husband, "How long was it before you stopped crying yourself to sleep?"

She couldn't tell me. But I cried every night for over a year. Now it happens less frequently.

One of the hardest things to do is to help people understand why I have no desire to seek out another relationship. I have well-meaning friends who've known me for over thirty years who think I should call an old friend (who had planned to ask me to marry him, but Danny asked me first). This man then married a very nice girl and they had two children and adopted two. She died from cancer about three years before Danny. And now this man is widowed. These well-meaning friends think I should call him. But I can't. How can I think of starting another relationship when I'm still in love?

Some people have asked me if I am mad at God. My reply is, "If God is my problem, there is no answer." I never was angry or upset with God. I did get angry with the doctor, but the Lord told me right away, being angry at her was not beneficial for me. So I chose to forgive her.

The Lord has been there for me through it all, and He has supplied my every need. He even worked miracles for me at my bank, the insurance company, and for my personal well being. Peace has been a daily blessing from the Lord. I can't praise Him enough for being there with me every step of the way. And I know He will be with me forever.

CHAPTER TWELVE

When a Parent Dies

Facing the death of a parent can leave one with a sense of the inevitable. Now is the time to understand you reign as a member of the next generation. It's also the time when you realize dependency on your parent(s) is now over. There will be no more discussions of the future, or conversations of the past. And no more answers to questions of ancestry. All advice has now been given.

Communication as it was has ceased. Your parent's life is complete, and over. This will be a different kind of shock. Although the death may have been expected, the reality of truth can be crushing. It most certainly will be a time of reflection.

THE NEXT GENERATION

We looked all around
at older ones together,
laughing with each other;
sharing memories of forever.

A few is all there is
to keep the family station.
When they are dead and gone
We are the next generation.

©Phoebe Leggett

Sometimes sorrow is delayed for the remaining parent as they try to protect and console their children. But when the truth hits, it can cause tremendous stress and anxiety for all involved. Plan to offer the remaining parent assistance when needed. And be prepared to take charge and help out. You must also remember to take care of yourself during the hours and days following the loss of a parent. This bereavement will affect not only you, but your siblings and the remaining parent, in unexpected ways. Allow God to be your strength and comfort as others reach out to you in sympathy and understanding.

SCARS

The scars of life
within—without;
but deep within
leaves not a doubt

to be the scar
that makes me mad;
that causes grief
and makes life sad.

A scratch, a bump,
a cut, a scrape
takes time to heal,
not time to make.

The scars of life
have left me broken;
have never mended
and are not spoken.

©Phoebe Leggett

If you are the adult child of a bereaved parent, your concern for that parent is essential. Realize that not only have you lost a parent, but your remaining parent has lost a spouse. They may need more understanding than usual. Often, a grieving mind will wander while struggling to overcome the loss of a partner.

The inability to concentrate while driving may become a dangerous activity for them, and for others. Often, the remaining parent is unsuccessful at staying focused while reading, eating, or watching television. But if their actions become bothersome to concerned family members, it may be time for someone to step up and take control of the situation.

A parent's failure to retain what they read or see can be overwhelming. As a caregiver, your patience will go a long way. Offer help with routine tasks, such as mowing the lawn or handling dangerous equipment, until your parent is able to again function in a normal way.

Unexpected bouts of crying, or the inability to handle sorrow may require more interaction from others. Depression and the lack of self-motivation may set in. Try to provide positive reinforcement for your parent, and contact a doctor if their emotional distress gets out of hand. Be aware of potential dangers, such as over usage of drugs and alcohol. Offer help and support when needed, and encourage your parent to express themselves verbally. Discussing their grief will help to ease their sorrow, and yours. Hopefully, and over time, a more positive outlook will emerge. Trust God for guidance as you and your parent overcome the sorrow of losing your loved one.

Having to dispose of a parent's possessions can be somewhat disturbing. Your childhood may come back to haunt you. Memories will surface that had long been forgotten. This can also be a time of resolution. Deciding to be the best you can be for the time you have left can be redeeming. Try to remember the good times as they will bring feelings of pleasure and sincere appreciation for your recently deceased parent. It can also be a time of re-thinking your own choices and desires. Admiration for your departed parent can establish your own determination to continue making your parents proud.

But if you had a strained relationship with a deceased parent, now is the time to forgive and move on.

My Dad

By Lori Marett

My dad was given six to twelve months to live. He divided that time up and lived another nine months. It was cancer. I pretty much said good-bye to him when he started losing his faculties. The man I saw two weeks before he passed was not my dad. The last week, he was comatose. So when the funeral came, I didn't cry. To this day, I have not wept for my father. I had a great relationship with him and knew he was whole again and in heaven. So I've not grieved the loss.

The rest of my family grieved, but I have not. Only a handful of times does a tear slip down my cheek when I think of something special we shared. But other than that, I rejoice at the passing of my father and can't wait to see him again. Now, if I were to lose one of my daughters to cancer, that would be a totally different story. For my dad, there really wasn't any grieving on my part. I know that probably sounds weird.

IN THE NIGHT SEASON

In the night season
I need a reason
to hold on.
It won't be long
'till He appears
oh, so near.
In the night season,
He is my reason
to live.

©Phoebe Leggett

Grieving My Mother

By Ann Tatlock

The call came early in the morning on August 1, 1985. As soon as I heard the phone ring, I knew who it was and what he was going to tell me. It would be my father calling long-distance from the hospital in Illinois, and he would tell me my mother had died.

Mom had been undergoing cancer treatment for eighteen months. Her death was not unexpected, and yet, when Dad told me she was gone,

I was devastated. Mom and I had always had a close, loving relationship; she was my confidant, the first person to whom I turned to share both the good and bad moments of my life.

The grief I experienced following her death ran deep, with all the usual feelings of loss and sadness. But at the same time, I experienced a certain restlessness I didn't expect and found it hard to identify. I often sensed that something was left undone; there was someone I needed to talk to, something I needed to say . . . and then I would understand. I simply wanted to talk with Mom, and she wasn't there.

Mom had been a constant presence in my life for twenty-five years, but all that was over now. We'd been separated by the finality of death. I wouldn't be talking with her anymore, not in this life, not until heaven.

But heaven, I realized, was the important thing. I was in one of those life situations where the rubber meets the road, where I couldn't coast by on merely empty words. My faith in God's promises had to be real, because God himself is real and good and unchanging. Did I believe in heaven? Did I believe that Mom, though she had died, was still alive in the very presence of God?

Yes. I did believe. And it was not a vague wish but a true knowing that Mom *still was,* and that though I couldn't see and be with her now, one day I would be with her again.

By this time in my life, I was a freelance writer of non-fiction articles, and I was working on my master's degree in journalism. With Mom's death, I felt compelled to find a new way to express both my grief and the hope I have in Jesus. I started writing my first novel, a fictional story based on Mom's experiences in the hospital.

That novel was never published, but it was a turning point in my career. I knew God was calling me in a direction I hadn't before considered: to use fiction as a vehicle for revealing truth, for telling about His plan of salvation and eternal life. Now, many years and several novels later, whenever a reader tells me a book of mine renewed her faith or inspired her in some way, I know God used my grief to put me in the position of passing hope on to others.

Remembering a parent's witty character in a humorous way can be another way of coping with their death. My mother would have enjoyed her great-granddaughter's fiasco at her funeral had she been alive to witness it. The innocent actions of a child can bring laughter to a grieving family even though the occasion may be very sad.

Tribute to Great-Grandmother

Standing in a reception line at her great-grandmother's funeral, seven-year-old Samantha was quite bored and very fidgety. As relatives and friends filed past, shaking hands or hugging family members, she realized she was also included in this strange and unusual ritual. Joining in, she firmly extended her small hand in anticipation of the next hand-shaker. Her countenance radiated with exuberance.

"Nana, tell those people over there to come over here and shake our hands," she said in a hushed tone as she pointed her finger at a small group huddled together while deeply engaged in conversation. Samantha then extended her hand to the lady next in line. "I saw you play the piano," she said. "I play the guitar."

The lady looked surprised as she shook Samantha's hand, as did others standing in line. It was obvious that Samantha had found her niche.

Following an appetizing luncheon provided by the church, the family then drove a short distance to the chapel at the Veterans Cemetery for the graveside service. While waiting for everyone to take their places, Samantha spotted some flags lined up at the front of the chapel. Allowing her curiosity to lead, she sprinted to the front and examined them at closer range. "Are these state flags?" she asked.

"No, those are Army, Navy, Air Force, and Marine, and that's the Christian flag at the end," Nana said in a whisper as she pointed to each one. Then, realizing Samantha needed something else to distract her and noticing the American flag nearby, Nana said, "Samantha, why don't you lead everyone in the Pledge of Allegiance? Then you can sit down because the pastor will be here in a minute to complete Great-Grandmother's funeral."

Unafraid and always ready to entertain, Samantha dashed to the podium and stood as tall as she could behind it. She lifted her small hands in a standing gesture and, with authority in her voice, asked everyone to stand. Placing her right hand over her heart she began reciting in perfect dialogue, "I pledge allegiance to the flag of the United States of America . . . "

Without missing a beat, everyone joined in, voices swelling with amazing American patriotism that gently echoed around the rock walls of the Veterans Chapel.

"What a patriotic way to complete a funeral service," Nana said to herself. "What better send-off could one get?"

After the funeral, as everyone filed out of the chapel, Samantha asked, "Grandpa, how did they get Great-Grandmother in that little box?"

As a way of explaining cremation to a child, her grandpa said, "They shrunk her down, and then put her in the box."

Still curious, Samantha asked, "How did they shrink her?"

"They put her in a big oven that made her shrink," Grandpa said, hoping this would be understandable to her.

"How hot was the oven?" Samantha asked with a curious look on her face.

"I don't know," Grandpa said.

Samantha thought for a minute. "Was it three hundred degrees?"

"Probably something like that." Grandpa grimaced, hoping this uncomfortable conversation would soon end.

"Oh, just like baking cookies." Samantha grinned, finally satisfied with his answer, and bounded toward the car and more interesting matters.

Losing My Parents

Both my parents were devout Christians, and raised their children with a firm hand. My father was the first to pass away. He was eighty years old when he died of cancer. He was buried at the Veterans Cemetery in Black Mountain, North Carolina, in honor of his military service. My mother passed away eleven years later, and was buried with him.

Although they lived through the Depression era, they didn't like to talk about it. My father served the military in both Army and Navy during World War II. While a sailor, he was shipwrecked and dumped into the ocean. Although he survived the cold and murky darkness of the water amid serious threats of shark attacks, he was forever changed. After the war, he remained edgy, nervous, and tense. Over time, he was unable to work a public job and became a full-time farmer.

My relationship with my father was minimal. He didn't want children, and remained somewhat aloof during my childhood. Although he required hard labor from his family on the farm, his input into my raising, other than teaching me the word of God, was almost nonexistent. Before he died, he did manage to say he loved me.

My mother read Bible stories and other books to me when I was small. But she loved the Bible best. Over time, her health deteriorated, and her final two years were spent in a nursing home. She died of a heart attack at the age of eighty-six. Her life was long—evidence that loving God had been her priority.

Both parents vigorously taught me the word of God. And they lived it. Because of them, I am a Christian today.

"Honor your father and mother—which is the first commandment with a promise—that it may go well with you and that you may enjoy **long life** on the earth" (Ephesians 6:2).

Epitaph written by Phoebe Leggett

Epitaph written by Phoebe Leggett

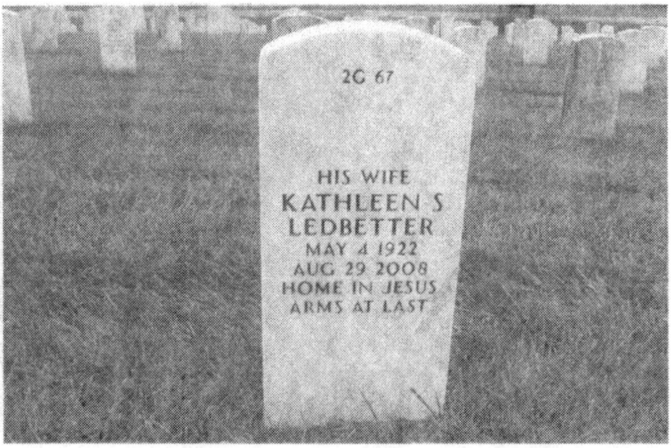

CHAPTER THIRTEEN

When a Small Child Loses a Parent

Following the death of a family member, everyone, including children, will feel incomplete and splintered as their world has now been shattered. The desire to withdraw from each other in order to address personal grief is normal. However, it's important that a child, or children, not feel disconnected from the rituals of death and burial. Try to stay connected with them, and address their grief in order to alleviate any fear they may have of the unknown.

Children need to talk about what has happened following the death of a parent. The ability to share their account with others can be therapeutic and healing. It's also important to listen to their words in order to validate their emotions. Over time, the child should have more understanding of a parent's death, and be able to move on with their life as time allows. Utilizing the same tools is also necessary if a child loses a sibling, or other significant family member.

Try to maintain daily routines with your child whenever possible. Inform schools, teachers, parents of friends, and other activity leaders of the death so they are aware, and can offer added support when needed.

Remember to share hugs and words of encouragement with your child several times a day. Allow them to communicate their own words of sorrow so they won't feel as if they're grieving alone. Request the help of other adults if your own sorrow becomes overwhelming. It's important that your child's needs are taken care of, even if by someone else.

A Child's Needs

- Explain to the child exactly what has happened, but in terms they can understand, and on their level.
- Help them acknowledge their fears concerning a parent's death, and show them how to overcome that fear.
- Offer constant reassurance so they can understand their parent's death wasn't their fault.
- Listen carefully to what they are trying to communicate to you.
- Realize your child is also grieving, and accept the way they are feeling.
- Do things that help them feel safe.
- Assist your child in understanding that others care how they feel.
- Remember to mention the deceased during holidays and special days so the child feels somewhat consoled following the loss.
- Continue to remember the parent who died by mentioning them each day in front of the child.
- Offer to pray with the child.

"But you, O God, do see trouble and grief; you consider it to take it in hand. The victim commits himself to you; you are the helper of the **fatherless**" (Psalm 10:14).

"'I will be a **father** to you, and you will be my sons and daughters,' says the Lord Almighty" (2 Corinthians 6:18).

"He defends the cause of the **fatherless** . . . giving him food and clothing" (Deuteronomy 10:18).

"I rescued the poor who cried for help, and the **fatherless** who had none to assist him" (Job 29:12).

"A father to the **fatherless**, a defender of widows, is God in his holy dwelling" (Psalm 68:5).

"The Lord watches over the alien and sustains the **fatherless** and the widow . . . " (Psalm 146:9)

"We have become orphans and **fatherless**, our mothers like widows" (Lamentations 5:3).

"Do not oppress the widow or the **fatherless**" (Zechariah 7:10).

CHAPTER FOURTEEN

When a Sibling Dies

Whether you are close to your sibling or not, if they die, your sense of loss will be overwhelming.

Losing My Brother

By Brian Foley

I was in shock when I found out my brother Matt had been killed. I didn't want to think about it. I wanted to pretend it hadn't happened. But when I did think about it, I had feelings of deep remorse. I was sorry I hadn't been a better example for him. I regretted not allowing myself a closer relationship with him. And I felt great sadness that I would never again have another chance to do things differently.

My guilt, for the most part, has been over allowing unimportant things to take the place of quality time with him. Although I had many memories running through my head after Matthew died, I couldn't concentrate on any one of them. I just wanted the bad news to go away. And to this day, I live with regret over things I could have done differently with my little brother. Before he died, I didn't understand what the consequences of losing him would be. But now I do.

Understanding the Death of a Sibling

It's hard to comprehend life without someone you grew up with, shared ordinary days and unique moments with, and enjoyed holidays and vacations with. But now the reality of a sibling's death is sinking in. Grasping the veracity that you both shared the same parents, values, and friends can make one understand how lonely it can be. The sheer sadness of a sibling's death will make that reality unbelievable, harsh, and unrelenting.

Now is the time to allow friendships to be your support as you grieve. Meeting others who share like compassions will be helpful as well as restorative. Sharing memories of the past can bring laughter and related understanding as ways are discovered to grieve, and heal, from your loss.

MISSING YOU

All these many new inventions
would have had all your attentions

as things have changed so drastically,
you would have loved fantastically.

When, only six short years ago,
you were alive and in the flow.

But now those years are in the past.
Yet, grief and sadness seem to last.

As heartache leads to sudden rage
huge teardrops fall upon this page.

I'm angry for your sudden death,
for you were full of life, and breath.

The things you missed, after you died,
fracture my heart so I have cried.

You thought you were invincible.
But death came, unpredictable.

Your wrong mistake became your err.
Misjudgment was your final snare.

Realizing a deceased sibling no longer has a future on this earth is a reality that will be heartbreaking for years to come. The loss of opportunity, the regret of promises made and not kept, and the useless waste of time can be staggering as the hopelessness of reality sinks in. Sudden sadness may overtake your senses. You can feel shame after realizing you could have been a better brother or sister. Conflicting thoughts and emotions will be confusing in the aftermath of a sibling's death. The sadness may linger and become frustrating as well as depressive. *What if things had happened differently? I can't believe he's dead. What if?*

SADNESS

After the sun has set,
after the day is gone,
I'm left at last to think
all by myself alone.

Deep sadness overtakes me
and tears begin to flow.
The storm is just beginning
and I am feeling low.

Your face then comes before me.
The past is all I know.
But you are in my future,
and I can't wait to go.

For there you are so happy,
not like you were before.
Quiet peace is all around you.
No fighting like at war.

Everything is clear and new.
It is as it should be.
And nothing else can matter,
for you have been set free.

©Phoebe Leggett

The significance of mortality can overtake your mind. The sudden ache of sorrow and the sharpness of disappointment may surface when you realize you will never again see your loved one alive. This emotion can be devastating. Acute horror at death's reality—the completeness of life—may be overwhelming. The truth of existence as it was has now become strange and unreal, even scary. Pondering what one could have done differently will reignite the grieving mechanisms all over again.

MYSTERIES

Mysteries I'll never know—
the crash that ended his life.
The pain he must have felt
on that awful, rainy night.

His troubled life near over,
Was he full of anger and strife?
His thoughts . . . were they on the Lord
on that awful, rainy night?

Did he realize the outcome?
Did he even try to fight
as his life was almost over
on that awful, rainy night?

He was by himself, alone.
The wrecked car held him tight
as his mind was surely racing
on that awful, rainy night.

One shot into the night.
Ambulance and police alike
showed up to give assistance
on that awful, rainy night.

The emergency staff imperfect
as they tried to do things right
and worked so hard to save him
on that awful, rainy night.

But he took his final breath
and stepped into the light.
He left us all so empty
on that awful, rainy night.

Anger and remorse may set in. Grinding memories of raw hurt and disbelief can be hard to deflect. All of a sudden you may realize you're the lone survivor, and begin to blame yourself. Feelings of guilt for being the one who's left standing can be staggering.

Survivor guilt is a common emotion, making it easy to accuse yourself. Harsh feelings of regret may surface. But blaming yourself is a distorted mindset that can be damaging, and should not be considered at any level. These emotions may be especially true if a sibling was young.

Brothers and sisters have a special type of relationship. The years spent together while growing up allow them to learn everything possible about each other. A lifetime of competition has likely strengthened that relationship. Learning the give-and-take of life has uniquely bonded you and your sibling together. Fighting, loving, teasing, defending, and hating each other is all part of growing up together. But when your sibling dies, that tie is forever broken, and a part of you will always be missing.

Forgotten Survivors

Siblings of a brother or sister who has died are often the forgotten survivors. It doesn't matter the age of the one who's left. The hurt is almost always the same. When a sibling passes away, the children that remain are often overlooked by parents, friends, or other relatives in the family. Parents who are grieving for themselves often forget that their other children are also dealing with sorrow. Or they may feel a need to protect them from the emotions of losing a sibling. In reality, parents need to understand that the death of their child will strongly affect the remaining children.

When a sibling dies, those left behind, no matter the age, are considered secondary mourners to spouses, parents, or the children of the one who has died. Children still living at home will take second place as the dead sibling takes prominence. He or she may emotionally lose their parents for a time as they grieve the death of the deceased child.

If the death was a suicide, the surviving siblings' role in the family may become altered. Children often feel protective of their parents, or the parents may try to shield their living children, no matter the age, as they become fearful of losing them also. Therefore, sibling survivors can become the forgotten mourners.

People often forget the importance of a sibling in their lives. The bond with a brother or sister during childhood is unique and special. Their longest relationship in life is almost always with a sibling. But when one dies, extreme anxiety often surfaces as a result of the close relationship they shared during a lifetime together.

This connection is usually the longest relationship shared with anyone. Because siblings are just a few years apart in age, they will know each other longer than spouses, parents, or even their own children. Brothers and sisters often share more life events and life changes with each other than with anyone else. They have the same family, the same culture, the same religious beliefs, and the same material possessions. And, as children, they will teach each other how to communicate with everyone else, and how to function in society. Siblings will spend more time together in their earlier years than they will ever spend with their parents.

A child's reaction to the death of a sibling will establish the way they will always view death. Many fail to believe that children need to grieve, but they do. Because small children have a shorter attention span than adults, their sorrow and heartache may appear short in endurance as it will only surface for short periods of time. Their grief may cause headaches and other physical problems. Children are undeveloped, and may have difficulty coping with the loss of a sibling. For them, it can be difficult to know how to express their sorrow.

Children are very aware when someone close to them has died, especially if it's a brother or sister. Even very young children realize that death brings loss and sadness. Although small in stature, a child has feelings that need to be addressed. Don't ignore their sentiment while trying to deal with your own. Children go through the grieving process in much the same way as adults.

GREATLY MISSED

He stepped into our lives.
The time was oh so brief.
At such a tender age,
he left us with such grief.

He died one rainy night.
Rain and tears were mingled then.
Lost control and lost his life.
No one knows just how or when

he entered Heaven's gate.
So young and yet no voice.
His time had come to go.
There was no other choice.

He went before we did.
This was a brand new twist.

This never should have happened.
He will be greatly missed.

©Phoebe Leggett

When a younger child dies, the surviving children may feel abandoned. Their need for affirmation is critical. They also need to understand that they are not dying themselves. All these changes will be confusing if their needs aren't attended to. Try to remember that they have emotions too. Allow the child to discuss their thoughts in depth as it will help lessen the severity of their hurt. Understanding what has happened will ease their pain, and make the death easier to accept.

Talk to survivors in a language they will understand, and respond to. If they're very young, use words they can comprehend. If older, use language they can identify with.

MATTHEW'S POND

Come on, let's go down
and visit Matthew's Pond.
We'll search for hidden treasures
inside nature's wand.

We'll watch 'mud puppies' swim
while catching fish galore,
and dig for unseen riches
at imagination's store.

Because his world of fun
lived deep beneath the water,
he netted lots of swimmers
and tanked them all together.

He loved all lakes and streams
with creatures he could tame.
And so we named this pond
in honor of his name.

©Phoebe Leggett

The truth of youth is doing things without considering the outcome. Having fun is the name of the game. It doesn't matter what others may say, the young will leave their mark in every corner of your world. And if they die, those corners will still be there, abandoned—but waiting in silence for you.

SILENCE

He was good with guitar strings.
A talented son was he.
New lessons gave him rhythm
but gifted notes were free.

At every music store he went
he gathered guitar picks.
They showed up everywhere he was.
He boasted quite a mix.

His anger played right through the strings
as he strung his notes with violence.
But now that room's forever still,
and echoes from the silence.

©Phoebe Leggett

CHAPTER FIFTEEN

When a Friend Dies

When Lazarus died, Jesus was so overcome with sorrow that He cried. There wasn't any doubt in His mind that His friend would live again. And yet, He couldn't stop the tears from flowing. Jesus felt the same emotional anguish of grief that we feel following the death of someone dearly loved.

Losing My Best Friend

As a child growing up in rural North Carolina with very few neighbors, I was blessed to have a friend nearby that was close to my age. Bonnie lived across the street, and we spent many happy hours together. The woods behind us were our extended playground. When we engaged in "playing Indian," our wigwams were built from broken tree branches found throughout the wooded area. Moss growing in abundance on the forest floor became our pretend beds. And our children were treasured dolls and fuzzy kittens dressed in faded baby clothing.

When other playmates visited, they would be our traveling companions. Hours of imaginative play developed as we tramped down a well-worn walking path to what we called "the Mica Mine," a small dugout cave near our home where the mica mineral was abundant.

As best friends, Bonnie, my brother, and I generated many hours of treasured memories together.

MY BEST FRIEND
To Bonnie

You were my best playmate,
and my favorite friend.
Alone we were nothing,
but together we could win.

Always with each other,
as children we would share
our snacks and treasured toys.
And we always played with flair.

Forever sharing secrets,
we bonded as a twin.
You were like my sister,
my playmate and my friend.

Dreams were for a lifetime,
a motto yet unspoken.
Our friendship was a pledge
and never to be broken.

We'll always be as one,
my playmate and my friend.
No one can separate us.
Our friendship has no end.

In warmer weather, Bonnie and I played together in my daddy's corn crib, creating a cozy home-like environment for ourselves and our babies. Hide-and-Go-Seek, Ain't-No-Bears-Out-Tonight, and Rock School were the games we played over and over again. Many hours were spent rolling down the hill in freshly mowed grass. And, as we grew, our relationship flourished, and Bonnie became the sister I never had.

When autumn arrived, we could be found playing in bales of hay stored in my daddy's barn. We spent many formative hours pretending to be housekeepers, mothers, and wives. A Saturday afternoon ball game in the yard wasn't unusual, and was very satisfying when played with my brother and other visiting friends.

Although climbing a steep hill near the church was tedious, it was worth the hike as we tramped through the cold snows of winter. The reward was sliding back down over the frozen, icy snow in washtubs and worn-out sleds.

As we matured, fixing hair and applying makeup became more important than childhood games. Boyfriends had to be considered, and teenage issues discussed in depth. Sharing hopes and dreams with my best friend remains a treasured memory from my youth.

Years later when Bonnie was diagnosed with uterine cancer, she renewed her trust in God as her primary source of strength. It was imperative that she had His arm to lean on through her diagnosis, cancer therapy, and ultimate resignation to dying. The others who supported her became her lifeline of hope until she died.

"God is our refuge and strength, an ever-present help in trouble" (Psalm 46: 1).

PUNCHING THE WIND

I knew life could get hard.
Sometimes it left terrible wounds.
But I didn't think *this* would happen.
When it did, I kept asking, "Why me?
There were no answers.

Sometimes I wanted to cry out loud.
I wanted to blame someone.
I wanted to lash out,
to scream and wildly wave my arms.

I wanted to shout, "It's just not fair!"
But that got me nowhere.
That got me nothing.
It was like punching the wind.

And then I cried out, "Lord, help me.
Please help me through this."
And He did.

©Phoebe Leggett

There was nothing more I could do for my friend except lend an ear and my sympathies. Although powerless to help, I knew she rested in God's hands. That was my only comfort.

Because of prior difficulties, Bonnie's delicate surgery had to be performed at Duke University Hospital in Durham, North Carolina. Following surgery, the doctor declared her cancer free. But a few weeks later, she began having complications and increasing pain. Her surgeon continued to insist she was cancer free although she suffered intense pain. At some point she was able to get a second opinion. The new doctor prescribed a pain management regimen when he discovered she wasn't cancer free after all. By this time, the disease had spread to her lungs and liver.

Bonnie realized that her surgeon had been overconfident and somewhat arrogant as he refused to accept the facts. Her cancer had not completely been removed, but had spread. It would have been easier had he acknowledged his mistake and offered an apology for the mismanagement of her disease. Because of his lack of concern, Bonnie wasn't re-treated in time to save her life. Although she began another regimen of chemo, the cancer was winning.

Ashen and frail, she continued her struggle to survive. The last time I saw her alive, she asked me to write her saga. And, with this narrative, I'm fulfilling her desire to have her story told.

In my eyes, Bonnie was a hero. With grace and dignity, she maintained her poise and composure during her ongoing battles with terminal cancer.

THE COMFORTER SAYS

I will hold you in your sorrow.
Give to Me your grieving heart.
All your strength will come from Me.
Peace from you will not depart.

I am strong and I will keep you.
Lean on Me with all your might.
You don't have to fear or worry.
I will help you win this fight.

Life has hit you fierce and hard.
It's a test to bring you near.
I will hold you close to Me.
You will no more have to fear.

I am with you as you grieve.
Place your lonely hand in Mine.
I will calm you with My peace.
It's a promise for all time.

©Phoebe Leggett

Bonnie spent the final months of her life reliving the triumphs of a successful marriage, and the accomplishment of being a mother. But the disconcerted hurts in her life had to be negotiated, and laid to rest. Remorse and anger surfaced many times as she battled numerous demons while struggling to forgive.

As Bonnie's sounding board, I spent many exhaustive hours listening to her grievances and concerns. She detailed unrelenting distress over terminal cancer and her impending death. Scores of narrative included comprehensive words of hope, listless expressions of despair, and ultimate resignation to the truth of her fate. Although Bonnie lived with expectation for a cure, and faith in God, she knew she may not survive her war. She was a fighter, and struggled to the very end as she wrestled with medications and harsh treatments. Because her family needed her, it was worth every effort taken to extend her life.

ANOTHER TIME—ANOTHER PLACE

Another place, another time,
you were always on my mind.
Childhood makes for innocent rhyme,
another place, another time.

Memories blocked by fewer lines;
the past you think of many times.
You were so sweet. You were so kind,
another place, another time.

Life passes by in certain time.
The years go fast and then you find
youth far away and then you say,
another place, another way.

You dream of love and then you find,
uncertainty of a different kind.
Innocence gone, but love remains
another place, but not the same.

So quick you passed.
Death did replace
the life you had,
it was a trace

of another time, another place.

Fifty-one is young by many standards. And yet, when Bonnie realized that death was closing in on her, she conceded and began to plan her own funeral. It seemed to ease her mind as she utilized her last weeks of life in expectation of her final departure. Her husband and son helped her choose the perfect burial plot at the cemetery. She prearranged her committal at the funeral home of her choice. And the church service was planned, songs selected, and speakers chosen. Everything was designed in minute detail. The pallbearers would be her son's Boy Scout troop, and her beloved horse would be saddled in a gorgeous blanket of funeral flowers in her honor. And it was so.

The detailed serenity of the memorial service coupled with a decorative graveside interment concluded the final chapter of my best friend's life. It was a serene and beautiful ceremony conducted in honor of daughter, wife, mother, and friend as she had planned. Her consideration for her loved ones was accomplished in elaborate detail.

Bonnie and I shared many secrets throughout the years. I miss my friend. Our childhood together created a unique bond between us. Throughout the years we remained close, and continued our friendship until death took her away.

MEMORIES

All that's left are memories
restored in picture form
as I sleep.

Dreams of a happier past,
free from the knowledge
that life is passing me by . . .

unconscious and unaware
that grief exists
after all.

©Phoebe Leggett

He Held My Hand is a book written by Deborah Morocco Mason that details her personal battle with cancer. Several years ago Deborah graciously signed a copy for me when we attended her church, The North Church, a Charismatic house of worship located in Dallas, Texas. When Bonnie shared her diagnosis with me, I handed her a copy of the book. That volume became her lifeline of hope as she battled her own disease.

Before she died, Bonnie ordered copies of the book, and had them delivered to her cancer treatment facility to be shared with other cancer patients. Her concern for others remains a legacy.

CHAPTER SIXTEEN

Possessions

Keeping a personal possession of the deceased as a token of remembrance is a wonderful way to help alleviate the pain of losing them. Family members, relatives, and friends who are given the opportunity to keep an article that once belonged to their loved one is a kind gesture for the grief-stricken. Many received items have become favored heirlooms over time. Memories are often attached to things that have been passed down from generation to generation to become a memorial of the departed.

Great-Great-Granny's old biscuit bowl carved from a tree by Great-Great-Grandfather is a unique commemorative from the past. An antique dresser or weathered kitchen cabinet can be incorporated into your living space as a way of alleviating your sorrow. Receiving an item that belonged to the deceased will allow feelings of closeness to remain. Retaining items for historical redemption can be another way of connecting with the past in a soothing way.

Keepsakes such as ashes in an urn placed on the mantle, or a favorite picture of the departed can inject precious memories that help to heal the heart. An old chair, a unique piece of clothing, or a beautiful piece of jewelry can provide consolation to a family member. Even old cards and letters can bring some aspect of closure to the pain.

When my son's few belongings were placed in my hands following his death, uncontrollable tears of grief rolled down my face and splashed onto the floor. Matthew's wallet was a personal part of him, and a much-remembered item. How many times had I seen him reach for it, and then return it again to his back pocket? Sometimes his wallet was so full his pant pockets sagged from the weight. This important article was his personal filing cabinet where notes, cards, and mementos were stored. Money wasn't the primary objective for this leather container. But the wallet was, without a doubt, an intricate part of his personality.

I fingered Matthew's wallet, when handed to me, with overwhelming emotion that was almost sacred. Raw sensations and a renewed realism of truth boggled my mind when I realized that just hours earlier this cherished piece of leather had been in Matthew's back pocket, and next to his breathing body.

TREASURES

My mansion is in heaven
not anywhere on the earth.
This treasure is forever.
Just go and count the worth.

With streets of purest gold,
and gates of priceless pearl;
a mansion built for me
much larger than this world.

Who would want to wait
for this world of bliss?
Who would count the cost too high
that they would want to miss?

Many people like to build
their mansions on this earth
while thinking that it proves
their monetary worth.

My treasures are in heaven
where thieves can't steal away
and moths cannot destroy,
but will be mine one day.

You may want to stay
but I am ready to go.
I want to see my son
and others that I know

in heaven, just inside
with Jesus by the gate.
I'm ready now to go
and I can hardly wait.

The Bible says my heart
is where my treasures be.
So, I'm going to my treasure
and spend eternity.

©Phoebe Leggett

"For where your treasure is, there your heart will be also" (Luke 12:34).

"Do not store up for yourselves treasures on earth, where moth and rest destroy, and where thieves break in and steal. But store up for yourselves treasures in heaven, where moth and rust do not destroy, and where thieves do not break in and steal" (Matthew 6:19, 20).

At some point following the death of a loved one, the question of what should be done with their personal belongings will surface. However, there's no set time to make this decision. It may take months, even years, before that issue can be addressed. But when you're ready, be prepared for renewed sorrow and grief.

What treasured memento will you keep for yourself? Are you willing to share with family or friends? Perhaps you aren't prepared to let go of anything. Will you ever? These are questions that will need answers at some point in the future.

Realizing others could benefit from a loved one's clothing or personal items is a step in the right direction. Holding on to material things could paralyze the grieving process. But when things are shared, perhaps with those in need, the willingness to release them will also assist in letting go of your loved one.

CHAPTER SEVENTEEN

Nightmare of Reality

"But the fruit of the Spirit is love, joy, peace, patience, kindness, goodness, faithfulness, gentleness and self-control. Against such things there is no law" (Galatians 5:22, 23).

It was difficult visiting the funeral home just to see the battered, bruised, and crushed body of my youngest child with my own eyes. Because Matthew was my baby, the pain of grief was unbelievable. When I entered the staged room where he was, I became numb.

His body was stiff and silent. His swollen head oozed a slow stream of blood, evidence of a recent trauma. And the metal slab where he lay was cold and rigid. He was as he had died, not yet prepared for burial.

I wanted to touch him and hold him close, to cradle him and tell him how sorry I was this had happened—that he deserved better than this. I wanted to tell him how much I loved him, that our past conflicts weren't important, but that *he* was, and that—somehow—everything would be alright. But I didn't, and it wasn't.

I just stood stone-cold in front of him, unable to move, unable to think, and unable to cry. I didn't want to believe this was my child. His arms were lifeless, his face immobile. His eyes were closed, closed by the funeral director for my viewing. His head was turned sideways, and his mouth was open as if asleep.

I wanted to shake his arm and tell him to get up. I needed to lift him off that cold slab and say, "What are you doing? You have your life to live. Get up, and live it."

I leaned over and touched his arm, and then his hand. They were cold and stiff, not warm and yielding. This wasn't the Matthew I'd given birth to, raised, and then released into adulthood. But it *was* him. This was unreal, unbelievable, and harsh.

But Dana, my husband, stood by my side, concern written all over his face.

I was stunned and dazed at the same time. This was too much to comprehend, so I put my thoughts and feelings aside for later when I could dissect them, one by one. It was hard to understand what my bewildered eyes had observed.

Later I would relive each moment, second by second, minute by minute. But for now, my tortured mind could not completely grasp the truth. These were moments best left for another time.

We confirmed our instructions with the director of the funeral home, and then drove to the home of my former in-laws, where Matthew had been living. Although it had been years since we had been together, their arms opened in sympathy and understanding as they grieved with us. Again, it was surreal.

The following day we traveled back to the funeral home with my son Brian. Once in the room, he stared, unreserved, at his brother positioned on the cold slab. He remained in stark silence for several minutes, his index finger resting on his chin, deep in thought.

The funeral service was planned for Saturday of that same week. My former brother-in-law would officiate. Somehow, everything fell into place as God provided ministers, a church, and everyone needed for the funeral and graveside rights. It was a miracle that so many caring people responded to our tragedy.

Earlier that year my husband's new employer moved us Charlotte, North Carolina. In order to find new friendships and a place of worship, we began attending an upstart but growing ministry. Although small in number, the possibilities of fellowship appeared strong. However, when our son died, the founder and pastor of this small church suddenly became unavailable. It was obvious his ministry didn't include assistance for the bereaved. But God, Jesus, and the Holy Spirit traveled with us, stood beside us, and comforted us through the most horrific and traumatic moments we had ever faced.

But, in retrospect, the support of the Trinity was all that really mattered.

When someone close to you dies, it doesn't take long to find out who cares and who doesn't. Allow the unsympathetic to walk away. Holding on to someone who is indifferent, uncaring, and heartless is a waste of time.

WHY ME

Oh, Lord, please help me.
I know I'm falling fast
as dark is getting darker,
and I'm alone at last.

Who sees and understands
I'm sinking in despair,
when nothing more is right,
and life seems so unfair?

But why, oh Lord, why me?
Why'd this happen to me?
My heart is crying out
and longs to be set free.

I'm feeling so alone,
yet people are around.
I'm drowning in despair,
yet making not a sound.

©Phoebe Leggett

The church where the funeral took place was full of compassionate ex-family members and friends of the family. Several ministers from the area were in attendance, including Rev. Doyle and Cheryl Marley, pastors and friends of the family whose former church was made available for the funeral. Former friends from my past also came, offering condolences and continued prayer for our family.

My prayer for three years had been that God would restore my family, and that Matt would be saved no matter the cost. The miracle: The family restored to me was my former in-laws. And, I have to believe my son received his salvation before he died. God answered my prayers, not in the way I thought He would, but in the way He knew was best.

The Funeral

Strained harmony of piano and organ drifted in melodious refrain through the doors of the Stoneville Pentecostal Holiness Church on Saturday, August seventh—the dreaded day of my son's funeral. My former brother-in-law, and pastor of a sister-church, led the family processional through wide, double doors and into the sanctuary. A melancholy hush settled over the crowd as we stumbled our way to reserved seats in front.

I glanced around the room, my heart pounding explosions of disbelief with each measured throb. *How could this be? No, this isn't just any funeral. This is my son's funeral.* I couldn't get my mind around it. I repressed tears that were on the verge of spilling down my cheeks. Stoic but terrified, I faced the reality of my truth, the finality of life as it had been. This was it—the final good-bye.

A former sister-in-law stood in front of a packed auditorium and began to sing "It Is Well with My Soul." The harmonious ebb and flow of her words, although soothing, was laborious to hear as it defined the finalization of death.

Matthew's uncle stood in front of family and friends and delivered a painful eulogy over his nephew. But I couldn't focus on his words as memories of Matt's childhood flashed before my eyes. His boyish giggles as he handed me a bouquet of wilted wild flowers . . . his twinkling blue eyes and tiny freckled nose . . . the first time I held him after nine months of feeling him move inside of me.

"A woman giving birth to a child has pain because her time has come; but when her baby is born she forgets the anguish because of her joy that a child is born into the world" (John 16:21).

"When you send your Spirit, they are created . . . when you take away their breath, they die and return to the dust" (Psalm 104:30, 29).

BREATH OF LIFE

God gave you breath
when you were born,
that gave you life
that ear morn.

God breathed it out
and gave to you
the breath of life
when you were new.

With it was given
all you would need
to live and love
and to succeed.

And when you died
that lonely night,
your soul then left
and took its flight.

When you exhaled
with your last breath,
God took it back
into himself . . .

the breath of life.

©Phoebe Leggett

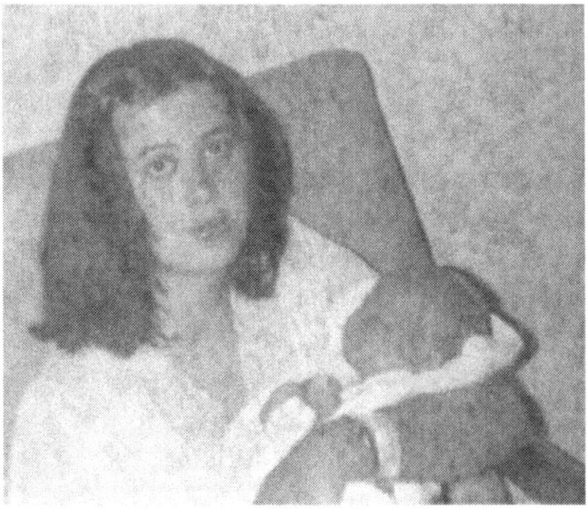

Phoebe holding newborn Matthew

Matthew was born at 1:02 early Monday morning, May 10, 1982. Labor began around 11:45 on Sunday evening, just before Mother's Day ended. Matt, an eight-pound, twenty-one inch baby, hurried into this world following a brief labor of just forty-five minutes. Although he was two weeks overdue, he made up the time with a speedy delivery.

As a child, he also generated a pattern of waiting—waiting until the last minute to finish homework, leave his play, or get dressed for school. When he was late, he would rush, or speed up, to recover the time. Even just before death, he retained that same pattern.

I can't stand it. I cannot handle this. I wanted to run away, but was too numb to move. Although the service pressed forward, for me the hands of time had stopped.

Following a heartbreaking service, relatives and church family came forward to extend hands of friendship, offer condolences, and share embraces of understanding and love. I was honored and humbled by the abundance of caring people who took the time to attend Matthew's funeral, and to acknowledge our grief. Again, it was surreal.

Several more of Brian's friends traveled from Tennessee to be with him and our family as a tribute to our loss. Throughout the course of the day they remained close by our side. Their presence generated needed emotional support. They will always be remembered for their kindness.

The Memorial

A memorial was held for Matthew at Brigman's Funeral Home in Black Mountain, North Carolina, a week following the funeral service. Since the interment was held many miles from where Matt grew up, it seemed appropriate to have his memorial service, and burial, in the town where he had spent most of his childhood. Although the turnout wasn't large, the number in attendance was perfect for closure. Pictures of Matt's life were shared as were other memorials. Several childhood friends attended as did a former Sunday school teacher.

At the Graveside

The drive from the memorial service to the cemetery was long and tedious. Although short in distance, this ride would be Matthew's last. Following the rituals of burial, he would be laid to rest in the unyielding ground of Mountain View Memorial Park in Black Mountain, North Carolina.

In just moments, our family would wind its tearful way from parked cars down a trampled path to the cemetery plot where Matthew's ashes would remain. As we began our descent to the burial site, Brian asked to carry the bronzed Urn that held his brother's ashes. He held the urn with a tender hand, and gently stroked it with the other. His gesture displayed great emotion, and remains a loving memorial to his brother.

Mountain View Memorial Park

Randy Stone, Pastor of the Meadowbrook Free Will Baptist Church in Black Mountain, North Carolina, and my mother's pastor, officiated at the graveside burial. The sincerity of his words brought heartfelt consolation to our grieving hearts as we stood in a huddled mass of disbelief. How soothing to have a compassionate minister of the Gospel, faithful in his commitment to God, willingly bestow support and assistance without question or resolve.

And when I saw my best friend Bonnie at the gathering, I was comforted.

Not one word need be spoken. Bonnie's presence alone brought a measure of restoration to my confused and grief-stricken heart. When I recall that ominous day, unbroken memories include her standing in silence beside my son's grave, hands folded, with quiet compassion on her face.

And, just three years later at the same cemetery I stood in silence, hands folded in renewed disbelief and added sorrow as Bonnie, my best friend, was laid to rest.

REMEMBER ME

Remember me
and don't forget
my eyes of blue.
And even yet,

my hair has tints
of red and gold
or none at all
when shaved to bald.

Remember me
my heart is true.
My words are kind,
for I love you.

Remember me
when you are sad.
Remember me
when you are glad.

Remember me
when flowers die.
Remember me
and please don't cry.

Remember me
when days are cold.
Remember me
when you get old.

Remember me
and don't be sad
for I was glad
in your own life
to be a part.

And always know
I will remain
so very near
to you each day
within your heart.

©Phoebe Leggett

CHAPTER EIGHTEEN

Cycle of Life

People may surround you while you're grieving, but you're still alone. Grieving can be shared with a community, a church, an organization, a neighborhood, or with family and friends. But when it comes down to it, this is a personal matter. The emotional pain inside is real, and it's all yours. It's an ache that won't go away.

Most churches offer grief counseling within the walls of their own facility. Pastors, rabbis, priests, and clerics are prepared to offer their services when asked. Schools and other public organizations provide guidance counselors specializing in grief counseling or other resources that may help. Doctors and medical personnel have similar resources for encouragement and support, if asked. The newspaper can also be another resource for gathering information on grief.

The library provides various materials, books, and other media for the grief-stricken. Funeral homes and related services offer materials and help for those grieving the loss of a loved one. And, the Internet has websites and services for the bereaved. There's no reason to grieve alone. And there's no shame in requesting help, if needed, for managing sorrow.

MEMORIES

Today he would be twenty-five
if from that crash he did survive.
He would be here and still alive,
if he had not gone for that drive.

The graveyard holds no mystery,
for sadness follows misery.
His life is now a history
of memories ever haunting me.

I 'oft can hear his clear demand,
his trumpet blasting in the band,
his guitar vibrant in his hand,
while laughing loudly in the stand.

I long to see him here today
and celebrate just one more way
to touch and hug, and hear him say,
"I understand" and "It's okay."

And yet I don't quite understand
just why his short life had to end.
It is so hard to comprehend
that life on earth is just a lend.

It's just so hard . . .

©Phoebe Leggett

The Holy Spirit can be your Comforter. If you don't have His consolation, perhaps it's time to ask Jesus into your heart. Then you will feel the warmth of God's presence as though a warm blanket of compassion is covering you. The aura of the Holy Spirit will be your help, your strength, and your comfort.

"My Comforter in sorrow, my heart is faint within me" (Jeremiah 8:18).

After the death of my son, I found comfort in composing creative poetry that detailed my sorrow. Places of solace defined my days as words of comfort from the Bible consoled my heart. Paper was my easel, and the keypad my paint brush. Many hours were spent perfecting words that spoke volumes to my heartache and sorrow. Writing and re-writing to exactness was an acquired skill that provided comfort during the process of grieving. And by reading my own words, I found peace for my shattered heart.

The consolation of the Holy Spirit continued to surround me following numerous days of sorrow. When insecure emotions engulfed my spirit, God's love and reassurance revealed His peace as promised in the Bible. God was with me the very moment I learned my son had been killed. He was with me when I viewed my son at the morgue. And He was with me during the funeral and the long days and nights that followed. He's with me still, bringing sweet comfort that can only come from Him.

I did not go in my own strength, but with the endurance God gave. His reassurance wasn't visible, but was concrete and solid. God's infinite peace that passes all understanding, and is beyond comprehension kept me stable. Although this journey of grief has been a difficult road to travel, there is a future and a hope. By faith, I hold on to the truths written in the Word of God—the Bible—and the unfathomable love that continues to rain down on me, covering my heart and soul with compassion and healing.

THE PICTURE

I looked at pictures of the man
and really could not understand
that just a couple of months before
he was alive and living more.

Too young to die—too young to cry
too young to face eternity's sigh.
It breaks my heart almost in two
because his life on earth is through.

And yet he had no way to know
that he would die in a month or so;
within his picture, smiling shy
before we said our last good-bye.

He was so vibrant and so young
while living life and having fun.
No one could know, but the Holy One,
his race with death was soon to come.

So we remember life on earth
by viewing pictures from his birth
and travel through his life in print.
So sad it's over and is spent.

©Phoebe Leggett

The Circle

With the death of a loved one comes mourning, anguish, distress, gloom, depression, despondency, dejection, loss of hope, ache, desolation, despair, isolation, lethargy, aching, suffering, gloominess, and regret.

MAY 10, 2006

Today he would be
twenty-four.
But he is gone.
He is no more.

His stay on earth
was way too short.
Tears fall like rain.
Deep is the hurt.

©Phoebe Leggett

Time heals all wounds, or so goes the cliché. In reality, time doesn't heal every hurt. But the passing of time can make the pain easier to accept. There are some sorrows, however, that will never reach the completed stage of healing. At times, and when least expected, deep sadness will overtake the sorrowful. There's no set time for grief. When heartache comes, it's best to go with it. Allow those ruthless emotions to sweep over your soul. Don't hold back the tears. Tears can be healing.

A few days after my son was killed I visited the local Hobby Lobby just to find a tranquil place of solace. Christian music filters throughout the store on any given day, and provides a peaceful atmosphere where one can shop. In just minutes following my arrival, the theme song from my son's funeral began to play. Tears spilled from my eyes and plopped down on my chest. My grief was out of control, and I was drowning in my own sorrow.

Blinded by tears, and unable to hide or walk away, I just stood in the aisle and allowed my sorrow to flow. I thought I was alone. But the Holy Spirit was with me, comforting me with words of hope as the song resounded in my ears, *It is well with my soul.*

CHAPTER CLOSED

Life's chapter is closed.
The book has been written.
There is no new mystery.
No more will be hidden.

The chapters were short
to coincide with his life.
No more left to happen.
There'll be no more strife.

His story's been told.
All chapters are read.
The book has been shut.
No more will be said.

Life's chapter is closed
on life's mystery.
The story has been read.
His life now history.

©Phoebe Leggett

As time begins to heal the pain of sorrow, pleasure, joyfulness, happiness, delight, elation, wonder, resolution, and peace will return to your heart and soul.

"I am worn out from groaning; all night long I flood my bed with weeping and drench my couch with tears" (Psalm 6:6).

"My intercessor is my friend as my eyes pour out tears to God …" (Job 16:20)

"He heals the brokenhearted and binds up their wounds" (Psalm 147:3).

"But I will restore you to health and heal your wounds, declares the Lord" (Jeremiah 30:17).

It will take time to heal your wounds. But joy comes in the mourning, and peace will follow soon after.

"And the peace of God, which transcends all understanding, will guard your hearts and your minds in Christ Jesus" (Philippians 4:7).

Nothing can ever be the same following the death of a loved one, no matter the circumstances. And naught can alter one minute already lived. Emotions of today will reflect those from the past. Whatever happens in the future responds to the past and is remembered. And after a loved one has passed, sadness and grief will be in the undertones of everything that happens for a period of time, if not forever.

Thoughts and feelings will continue to be affected. Emotions of the past will sweep beyond and, with boldness, await you in the future. That mindset may fade with the passing of time, but can resurface when least expected to surround you with renewed sorrow and grief. Just know that when others no longer care, Jesus will.

HE IS JESUS

When you've just lost your best friend,
And that friendship had an end,
When your heart has much to mend,
there is Jesus.

When you're troubled with life's pain,
and there's much more loss than gain,
When your tears fall down like rain,
there is Jesus.

When you've done all that you know,
but the answers are too slow
Just reach out and you will know,
there is Jesus.

When you just slid hard and fell,
and there's no one you can tell,
When your plans just go to hell,
there is Jesus.

He is waiting just for you
with a love that is brand new.
He will see you make it through.
He is Jesus.

He will take your shattered dreams,
take your plans and broken schemes.
He will fix them by His means.
He is Jesus.

He will wipe away your care
Just reach out, for He is there.
All His love with you He'll share.
He is Jesus.

CHAPTER NINETEEN

Memories and Hope

The aroma of pizza covered in chunky toppings drifting past my nose reminds me of Matt's favorite food. Baseball caps, his favorite piece of clothing, are scrutinized as I wonder which one he would choose to wear. Every young man I see with a shaved head reminds me of my son. He was his own barber, and never failed to leave a sink full of scraggly strands for me to complain about. Today I would love to scoop them up in my hands. Once Matt even displayed a head full of blue hair. His bold choice of color created a huge sensation at school, and with his peers. The embarrassment I then felt, I now regret.

HEAVY HEART

If you could know
just how I feel;
although you're gone,
you are still real.

If you could touch
my heavy heart
and know my pain
from end to start.

If you will hold
eternity,
I'll be there soon;
just wait for me

©Phoebe Leggett

Drawing by Matthew Foley

God knows how it feels to lose a child. He also lost His Son through death. What greater example is there?

Many thoughts raced through my mind the day I learned of my son's death: the sweetness of his childhood, music vibrating from his guitar as he strummed the strings, a newborn baby in my arms. I was perplexed, and distraught, at the same time.

Where would I find the strength to endure what was in front of me?

God willingly allowed His Son to die. But was I ready to release mine? I couldn't understand the logic.

Many years were spent raising Matthew, caring for scraped knees, broken bones, and stitched cuts while loving him through it all. But those moments dimmed in light of the sorrow I now faced.

I had endured many hurts in life: twelve years of an abusive first marriage, a painful divorce, and the abrasive struggle of raising three children as a single parent on a limited income. Even a wonderful second marriage had its own set of problems. Being diagnosed with multiple sclerosis during this same period of time was another harsh blow. But having to bury my youngest was more difficult than all the suffering I had already endured, including a painful childhood.

Hadn't I suffered enough? My son's death was more than I could bear.

But I had to trust in God. There was no one else.

"Surely God is my salvation; I will trust and not be afraid. The Lord, the Lord, is my strength and my song; he has become my salvation" (Isaiah 12:2).

I THINK OF YOU

I think of you
when I see

fish in aquariums,
red Toyota cars,
guitars of all kinds,
jalapenos in a jar;

blue plaid shirts,
worn Reebok shoes,
Papa John's Pizza,
animals in a zoo.

Rivers and lakes,
water and streams,
critters in the wild,
you—laughing in my dreams.

I think of you
when I see

young men everywhere,
heads shaved like a dime,
running up the stairs,
taking two at a time;

a black Nissan Maxima,
like your first car;
young boys on skateboards,
Kit-Kat candy bars;

music playing loudly,
a funny TV show,
a hearty, roaring laugh,
backyard Wiffle ball.

The list goes on and on
of all the things I see
that makes me think of you;
and it always shatters me.

©Phoebe Leggett

Matthew was an incredible artist. As a child he was always scribbling on paper. Now those pieces of paper that survived childhood give insight to his artistic abilities. But the world will never know his forte, for his brilliance will never be realized, or celebrated.

Childhood Drawing by Matthew Foley

Matthew loved all wildlife, but fish, frogs, turtles, lizards, and other amphibians were his favorite. We expected he would study to be a scientist or biologist. But when he grew up, those plans were squashed as peer pressure drove him to the dark side. There had always been hope that he would change direction, and pursue a more productive lifestyle. But he died, and those dreams were forever crushed. The difficulty of accepting these terms has been a struggle.

As an avid reader, Matthew gained much of his knowledge by reading encyclopedias and watching scientific media on television. With a higher than average IQ, his range of knowledge surpassed most of his peers. But a common sense factor was missing, often described as his crossing the road before checking to see if it was safe. The clinical response would now be a diagnosis of Asperger's Syndrome.

When Matt became a young man, his desire to play the guitar surfaced. After just a few lessons, his exceptional talents were evident. He had a huge desire to own unique guitars and, over time, owned several. Every music store in his path was a reason to visit, sample, and strum to his heart's content.

Reflecting back on happier times has helped me understand how positive memories can help relieve the pressures of grieving. When I write poetry or short stories, I realize that Matthew's life was not in vain. The wonderful incidents that occurred when he was alive are worth repeating, and provide excellent fodder for journaling. In this way I can remember the past in positive ways.

Sharing memories as a family can bring healing and wholeness, as it allows needed support even though the circle is now broken. When grieving becomes serious, try to focus on other things. Or be selective with the memories that are worth retaining, and dwell on those. Change the thought pattern when contemplating a downturn to despair. Reflect on joyful moments from the past, and allow God to be your source of strength. Stay busy, and prepare for sorrowful moments with alternative reflections. Remember to make decisive efforts to defray unstable thoughts when necessary.

WOUNDS

Life's wounds take time to heal,
yet grief is all I feel.

God did not choose to kill.
My heart is broken still.

The future will reveal
that all was in God's will.

©Phoebe Leggett

"My life is consumed by anguish and my years by groaning; my strength fails because of my affliction, and my bones grow weak" (Exodus 15:2-4).

"The Lord is my strength and my song . . . " (Psalm 118:14).

"God is our refuge and strength, an ever-present help in trouble" (Psalm 46:1).

"Do not grieve, for the joy of the Lord is your strength" (Nehemiah 8:10).

DAY AFTER DAY

Day after day,
week after week,
month after month,
grief after grief.

Sadness and tears,
sorrow on sorrow;
grief overtakes me
like no tomorrow.

It never ends,
this emptiness inside.
Unexpected tears
without reason or rhyme.

Sorrow upon sorrow
and grief upon grief,
day after day
and week after week.

Month after month,
and year after year,
yet life goes on
with always a tear.

It never ends
this grief in my heart.
It's hard to believe
we both had to part.

©Phoebe Leggett

When we returned from the morgue, my daughter and granddaughter stayed the night at our home. The following morning Dawn drove to Greenville, South Carolina to meet her husband and finalize the purchase of their new home. After their acquirement, they spent a couple of days moving furniture into their new place as previously planned. This occupied her mind and helped to keep her focused. The funeral on Saturday would be her time to face the reality of losing her brother.

Samantha stayed with her grandpa and me until the funeral. Her birthday on Wednesday, and the days that followed, kept me occupied as I busied myself caring for her. In retrospect, this arrangement was beneficial as it helped to suppress my anguish. Her presence softened the crush of reality that would later shatter my heart into a billion pieces.

Brian arrived from Tennessee Thursday afternoon. His trip had consumed more than seven hours of time on the road. The environment was charged with sadness as we embraced with mutual understanding and sorrow. The gray sky outside echoed the somber emotions inside as everyone tried to rest and re-group. Meanwhile, Dana and I prepared for our return trip to the morgue that was scheduled the following day. Brian needed to see his brother before cremation, and visit with relatives before the funeral on Saturday.

Friday morning we rented a van to limit the number of vehicles needed for our ride to the funeral, and to be together under one roof. The service was planned for Saturday, which was the following day. The funeral, and everything it entailed, had to be done, and needed to be done. As horrible as it was, the ritual of a Christian funeral was required for closure, and as a testimony of God's covering.

Because our recent move to Charlotte hadn't produced a bounty of friends, James and Michael K., Brian's friends, provided diversion and support after they arrived from Tennessee to join us for the funeral.

DEATH CAME

Investments made
but for what?
Death came
and took the lot.

Removed life's plans
with the stories.
Left the memories
of life's glories.

Gone in a flash.
Wind swept away,
leaving behind
life's longest day.

Where did you go
before my eyes blinked
when your heartbeat stopped,
as death at you winked?

Who would have thought
that life was a lend,
'till death took it over
and it had to end?

©Phoebe Leggett

At his death, Matthew was employed and saving for college tuition. He was registered to attend school in the fall. The car he was driving was his own, and it was insured. And, he had been attending church on a regular basis.

There Is Hope

This is what the Lord says: "A voice is heard in Ramah, mourning and great weeping, Rachel weeping for her children and refusing to be comforted, because her children are no more." This is what the Lord says: "Restrain your voice from weeping and your eyes from tears, for your work will be rewarded," declares the Lord. "They will return from the land of the enemy. So there is hope for your future," declares the Lord. "Your children will return to their own land" (Jeremiah 31:15-17).

'Is not Ephraim (Matthew) my dear son, the child in whom I delight? Though I often speak against him, I still remember him.

Therefore my heart yearns for him; I have great compassion for him,' declares the Lord . . . " (Jeremiah 31:20)

"He will wipe every tear from their eyes. There will be no more death or mourning or crying or pain, for the old order of things has passed away." (Revelation 2:14).

A New Direction

What better way to grieve than to recall the good times shared with a loved one before they passed? Memories can help sort through the loss in a positive way. But when you realize the times spent with your loved are forever gone, feelings of sadness may be overwhelming. Now is the time to redirect your thoughts to happier moments from the past, and hold them close to your heart.

Joining others on the Internet through Facebook and other websites is the rage for sharing words of comfort while remembering a loved one. Reading written expressions of others who are also grieving can be remedial. Although it may take years to sort through the heartache of sorrow, having a place to remember a loved one in written word can be therapeutic, as missing them often takes center stage at unrehearsed moments. Birthdays and anniversaries of the deceased are often the occasions when raw emotions surface. Capturing happier moments or sifting through the rawness of grief in written form can be curative. Comforting words can bring remedial restoration as you celebrate your loved one's life in this way.

WINTER SNOW

Dedicated to my children, who were my inspiration

Winter snowing,
faces glowing.
Wind is breezing,
snowflakes teasing.

Shedders sledding,
noses freezing.
Snowballs rolling,
snowmen growing.

Time is fleeting,
daylight leaving.
Inside alluring,
cider brewing.

Fire is burning,
popcorn popping.
Day's not over.
Snow still calling.

©*Phoebe Leggett*

More Memories

Matthew loved to play outdoors, and spent much of his childhood in the various elements of rain, snow, and sun. Many hours were also spent on a rope swing while playing with siblings. Toy trucks were utilized as moments of sandy construction generated positive reinforcement for lengthy friendships. Neighborhood playmates were always welcomed—the more the merrier.

Gardner Dome Team

SUNDAY AFTERNOON BALLGAME

Dedicated to Brian and Matthew and the Gardner Dome Team

While folks are napping,
the kids are whacking.
The ball goes flying,
the dogs are yapping.

The scores are flashing,
the teams are gasping.
The game is going,
our team is winning;
the sport—never ending.

The leaves are falling,
our mom is calling.
The day is ending,
fun just beginning.

Friends are giving
and life is living,
but never forgetting,
Sunday afternoon ballgames
in my head always spinning.

©Phoebe Leggett

Matthew spent many hours with his brother and neighborhood friends playing Wiffle ball, football, and sledding in the backyard—whatever the season dictated. Summertime was made for soaking friends with a water hose when the sweltering heat required it. Even outdoor games, such as hide-and-go-seek, proved to be constructive exercise. The wooded areas beyond our yard gave protection while carrying toy guns and rifles to stave off pretend enemies.

The exuberance of childhood, full of laughter and energy, has emerged as pleasurable memories for all who were friends with Matthew. Observing the children at play will forever be etched in my mind, and worth taking the time to recollect. Peaceful moments when life was calm and happy are best preserved in pictures and journals.

THE SWING

The rope swing is empty
and sits all alone,
just waiting for you
to come on back home.

As wind blows it softly,
it spins, and it turns,
still waiting for you,
as autumn leaves burn.

The tree is now barren
as fall turns to cold.
A lonesome swing waits
for your hands to hold.

Stormy winter is harsh
as a blue 'Easter blows.
And snow hides the swing
as time slowly goes.

Warmer days whisper "spring"
as mockingbirds fly by.
But you're no longer here,
sailing high to the sky.

Even in summer,
when everything is bright,
there's no joy or laughter,
as dusk turns to night.

That swing was your treasure,
but now it sits there quiet.

CHAPTER TWENTY

Grieving the Loss of a Pet

Freddie the cat was Matt's personal pet. After his death, that cat became even more important to me. As unusual as it was, Freddie seemed to understand my sadness as he stayed close beside me when my grieving became critical, and out of control. Four years later he disappeared, and never returned. His disappearance created a new grieving pattern, as his absence brought renewed feelings of sorrow.

Although many years have passed since Freddie's disappearance, I continue to miss him. What was learned is that grieving the loss of a pet can be as consuming as mourning the death of a human being.

There will always be something to regenerate new pain and hurt caused by the loss of someone, or something, you've loved and cherished. It may be difficult to get beyond the sorrow, as the heart just won't cooperate. Although never easy, it may be necessary to put true feelings aside as other concerns challenge the issues of grieving. As Scarlett O'Hara once said, "I'll think about it tomorrow." When reflecting on sorrow becomes too raw, it may help to redeem the time by pondering those memories at a later time.

PERSONAL PAIN

Sometimes I feel so lost.
There seems to be no gain.
There is just a lot
of my personal pain.

His cat at the door
wanting to come in
brings back memories,
reminding me of him.

However strange it is
there's comfort in his cat,
as he rubs on my face
he says that "I know that."

Someone had to ask
if I am okay.
"Just some personal pain"
is all that I could say.

I put on "smiley face"
and go about my day.
But tears are just hiding
and won't go away.

CHAPTER TWENTY-ONE

Other Reasons to Grieve

It's difficult losing a child to drugs, alcohol, prostitution, or other influences in this world. It's hard to stand back and watch as your child disregards, and then discards parental love and positive training without a second thought. But when that child is of age, there's nothing more that can be done, as a parent, to prevent them from making immoral choices and wrong decisions. Pray for them, entrust their life to God, and believe that one day they will return home.

Bring Them Home

By Cindy Sproles

"Your children hasten back . . . 'Lift up your eyes and look around; all your children gather and come to you. As surely as I live,' declares the Lord, 'you will wear them all as ornaments; you will put them on, like a bride'" (Isaiah 49:17-18).

Sometimes we do for the good of the many at the cost of the one—even when that decision crushes our hearts.

My husband tightened the last screw into the lock. "This is our home. We shouldn't have to put locks on our door." He dropped the screwdriver back into his tool box and walked into our son's room.

"Box up his stuff. All of it. He's got to hit bottom before he'll change."

That night, every item I packed away was bathed in tears. Our child, lost. We had to push him away, turn our backs for a time, and pray that God would restore him.

Five years passed, two without any word, any news, or any knowledge. The rest were sporadic sightings of him from a distance. Shoving him away was the hardest thing we'd ever done; the sacrifice of the one for the health and safety of the rest of our family. God moved away from His children for a time, too. They had to hit bottom in order to be restored. Renovation isn't a pretty process. Walls are ripped down, wires uncrossed, foundations repaired. But God promised to refurbish, build up, and repair. He promised to bring our children, and his, back; to gather them around us. I prayed every morning this year that God would restore my family. *Bring our prodigal home to the arms of the parents who love him*. As Christmas approached, we heard he was on his way. But we'd heard this before, and he was always a no-show. Would he *no-show* again? Christmas arrived. Our door opened and there was our prodigal. Home. I gazed across the room at our four sons laughing together as though no time had passed. Not only had God restored our family, but He'd wiped away the hurt of memories past. Our home was filled with joy; and when the evening ended, I took a picture of our boys, gathered together, and placed it near my heart. *"You will wear them all as ornaments."* God is a God of restoration. He understands tough love and the pain it demands. But He delights in restoring your soul. Have you felt the sting of loss? What treasured relationship needs to be restored in the New Year? Let the Master Carpenter do His job.

Additional Reasons to Grieve

- Losing a job that for years had defined you
- Moving away from family and friends
- Trusting a friend who later betrayed you

- An injury or disease that changed your relationship with someone you loved
- Losing a home
- Trusting someone who later proved to be untrustworthy
- Bad health
- Sickness unto death
- Losing hope; depression
- Divorce

CHAPTER TWENTY-TWO

Reflection and Resolution

Reflection

One day, I noticed a bird flying too low in front of a speeding car. As I watched, the car whizzed past, and the bird fell with a thud to the road. When it didn't move from its place, I knew it had been killed. After a short moment, another bird flew to its side and stood for a long time, watching in silence as if grieving. I felt the bird's sorrow as it flew away, never to return. Its actions brought tears to my eyes. Somehow that bird knew its mate was dead.

THE MISSING PART

A part of me is missing
of flesh and blood and life.
My loved one I am grieving.
He died alone one night.

©Phoebe Leggett

If God sees a sparrow fall, how much more does He care when one of His own, His greatest creation, falls from this life? "How much more valuable you are than birds" (Luke 12:24).

WHO KNOWS

Who knows
the pain of cruel grief
a hollow broken heart
facing uncertain days
as lives are ripped apart?

Who knows
regret and raw despair
while trying to endure
the nights so long
when nothing seems secure?

Who knows
as guilt replaces reason;
day and night
becoming one
season after season.

Who knows
how harsh and how intense;
and who knows for how long
this heartache
has to last?

Who knows?
And who can understand
a life that is gone . . .
more than losing
one's best friend?

Who knows?
God knows.

©Phoebe Leggett

If a time of solace is needed to reflect on past memories, or to consider the future, a visit to the cemetery may be the key. But that stopover can be grueling. When I gaze at my son's grave marker through tears of sadness, I continue to mourn his death while considering all his unfulfilled hopes, dreams, and desires. Those quiet moments at the memorial park often bring a sense of closure, although upsetting at best. Pulling stray weeds that spring up around his grave marker provide a sense of purpose. Leaving seasonal flowers allow the nurturing part of motherhood to surface as I continue to care for the needs of my son. But most of the time, I leave in tears and a renewed broken heart.

My friend Bonnie is buried in a plot near my son. Sometimes I place a flower on her remains as a memorial to our friendship.

Visiting places a loved one enjoyed, and doing the things they liked to do, can help alleviate some of the sorrow. Completing an unfinished project for them may bring a sense of closure. And, sharing memories of mutual interests with relatives and close friends will also be restorative. When I drag out videos from Matthew's childhood, the pictures soothe my mind. Once again I can watch him laughing while engaged in joyful play. But other times, the sadness is overwhelming as I realize those days are gone forever.

Resolution

God doesn't play fair with those He loves concerning His promises. We don't understand why God operates the way He does. And we don't know what's just around the corner. But God does. There is, however, a spiritual covering over a household of faith. God's promises are true. If He promised to save a household, we must believe that those members will be saved.

The jailer called for lights, rushed in and fell trembling before Paul and Silas. He then brought them out and asked, "Sirs, what must I do **to be saved**?" They replied, "Believe in the Lord Jesus, and **you will be saved—you and your household**. (Acts16:29-31)

One of the criminals who hung there (on a cross next to Jesus) hurled insults at him: "Aren't you the Christ? Save yourself and us!"

But the other criminal rebuked him. "Don't you fear God," he said, "since you are under the same sentence? We are punished justly, for we are getting what our deeds deserve. But this man has done nothing wrong."

Then he said, "**Jesus, remember me** when you come into your kingdom."

Jesus answered him, "I tell you the truth**, today you will be with me in paradise.**"(Luke 23:39-43).

Even on a deathbed, the spoken name of Jesus can allow the dying to receive salvation. Believe that Jesus died on a cross, shed His blood for the atonement of sin, and returned from the dead to give life to all mankind. Faith is all that's needed to receive salvation, and forgiveness. To understand is to believe.

"Jesus said to the woman, 'Your faith has saved you; go in peace'" (Luke 7:50).

"We are confident, I say, and willing rather to be absent from the body, and to be present with the Lord" (2 Corinthians 5:8).

I had to make a critical but spiritual decision when my son Matthew died. Would I place blame on God for his death and travel down the road many had taken before me? Or would I continue to trust in the God of my salvation?

When I released my son to God, it was before he was born, and again when he was having difficulty as a young man. Matthew had been in the hands of God his entire life. I knew there was nothing I could do that would change his destiny. But God could.

Many prayers had been prayed for my son, for his salvation and his protection. In the eyes of man, I had a right to blame God for his death. But I laid the blame aside, and continued to trust.

God is often condemned when a catastrophe or unexpected death occurs. But is it fair to reprimand the only one who understands, and knows all things? God may have allowed a loved one to die a premature death just to secure their place in heaven. Perhaps the point of death was the only time a loved one's heart would be tender enough for them to accept salvation. There are even times when the early death of a loved one is the turning point for someone else. Who are we to judge the sovereignty of God? He alone knows the end from the beginning.

"Therefore judge nothing before the appointed time; wait till the Lord comes. He will bring to light what is hidden in darkness and will expose the motives of men's hearts" (1 Corinthians 4:5).

God did everything possible to purchase our salvation. He even allowed His Son to die in agony for the sin of the world. Why not believe that He would also do whatever was necessary to honor the prayers of parents, siblings, relatives, friends, and church members who had prayed in absolute faith for the salvation of a loved one?

"He (God) hears the prayer of the righteous" (1 Chronicles 16:11).

"The righteous cry out, and the Lord hears them; he delivers them from all their troubles" (Psalm 34:17).

"At the very time God had promised . . ." (Genesis 21:2)

"Record my misery; list my tears on your scroll—are they not in your record" (Psalm 56:8)

"You have collected my tears in your bottle. You have recorded each one in your book . . . You have kept count of my tossings; and put my tears in your bottle" (Psalm 56:8 NLT).

Overcome by an unrelenting need to offer prayers of intercession for my son, I knelt before God one Wednesday night a few days before he died. Words for his salvation and safety flowed from my lips as tears flooded the altar where I bowed. So deep was my prayer that my heart felt it would burst. In retrospect, there was a reason and a purpose. A few days later, Matthew was dead.

Just as Jesus prayed in the garden before His death: "Going a little farther, he fell with his face to the ground and prayed, 'My Father, if it is possible, may this cup be taken from me. Yet not as I will, but as you will'" (Matthew 26:39), God knew what was ahead for Matthew just as he knows what's ahead all for us.

"'For I know the plans I have for you,' declares the Lord . . ." (Jeremiah 29:11)

CHAPTER TWENTY-THREE

Bible Verses of Comfort

"Even though I walk through the valley of the shadow of death, (or through the darkest valley) I will fear no evil, for you are with me; your rod and your staff, they **comfort** me" (Psalm 23:4).

"When I was in **distress,** I sought the Lord; at night I stretched out untiring hands and my soul refused to be comforted" (Psalm 77:2).

"My **comfort** in my suffering is this: Your promise preserves my life" (Psalm 119:50).

"As a mother **comforts** her child, so will I **comfort** you; and you will be **comforted** . . ." (Isaiah 66:13).

"Do not let your hearts be troubled. Trust in God; trust also in me" (John 14:1).

"Who **comforts** us in all our troubles, so that we can **comfort** those in any trouble with the **comfort** we ourselves have received from God. For just as the sufferings of Christ flow over into our lives, so also through Christ our **comfort** overflows" (2 Corinthians 1:4, 5).

"Blessed are those who mourn, for they will be comforted" (Matthew 5:4).

"Ask and you will receive . . . " (John 16:24)

"Praise be to the God and Father of our Lord Jesus Christ, the Father of compassion and the God of all **comfort** who **comforts** us in all our troubles" (2 Corinthians 1:3).

"And the **peace** of God, which transcends all understanding, will guard your hearts and your minds in Christ Jesus" (Philippians 4:7).

"You will go out in joy and be led forth in **peace**; the mountains and hills will burst into song before you, and all the trees of the field will clap their hands" (Isaiah 55:12).

"Peace I leave with you; my **peace** I give you. I do not give to you as the world gives. Do not let your hearts be troubled and do not be afraid" (John 14:27).

"My **comfort** in my suffering is this: your promise preserves my life" (Psalm 119:50).

"He himself bore our sins in his body on the tree, so that we might die to sins and live for righteousness; by his wounds you have been **healed**" (1 Peter 2:24).

"Indeed, in our hearts we felt the sentence of **death**. But this happened that we might not rely on ourselves but on God, who raises the dead" (2 Corinthians 1:9).

"May the **God of hope** fill you with all joy and **peace** as you trust in him, so that you may overflow with **hope** by the power of the Holy Spirit" (Romans 15:13).

"Then he said, 'Jesus, **remember me** when you come into your kingdom'" (Luke 23:43).

"Jesus answered him, 'I tell you the truth, today you will be with me in **paradise**'" (Luke 23:42).

"Listen, I tell you a mystery: We will not all sleep, but we will all be changed—in a flash, in the twinkling of an eye, at the last trumpet. For the trumpet will sound, the dead will be raised imperishable, and we will be changed. For the perishable must clothe itself with the imperishable and the mortal with immortality. When the perishable has been clothed with the imperishable and the mortal with immortality, then the saying that is written will come true: '**Death has been swallowed up in victory**'" "Where, O **death**, is your victory?

Where, O **death,** is your sting" (1 Corinthians 15:54, 55)

Cremation

"When the people of Jabesh Gilead heard of what the Philistines had done to Saul, all their valiant men journeyed through the night to Beth Shan. They took down the **bodies** of Saul and his sons from the wall of Beth Shan and went to Jabesh, where **they burned them.** Then they took their bones and buried them under a tamarisk tree at Jabesh, and they fasted seven days" (1 Samuel 31:11). (Note: Because the fire wasn't hot enough to cremate bones, they had to be buried.)

"All go to the same place; all come from dust, and to dust all return" (Ecclesiastes 3:20).

Salvation and Healing

"Heal me, O LORD, and I will be **healed**; save me and I will be **saved**, for you are the one I praise" (Jeremiah 17:14).

"Jesus turned and saw her. 'Take heart, daughter,' he said, 'your faith has **healed** you.' And the woman was **healed** from that moment" (Matthew 9:22).

"The grass **withers** and the flowers **fall**, but the word of our God stands forever" (Isaiah 40:8).

"In this you greatly rejoice, though now for a little while you may have had to suffer **grief** in all kinds of trials. These have come so that your faith—of greater worth than gold, which perishes even though refined by fire—may be proved genuine and may result in praise, glory and honor when Jesus Christ is revealed" (1 Peter 1:6, 7).

"For none of us lives to himself alone and none of us **dies** to himself alone. If we live, we live to the Lord; and if we **die**, we **die** to the Lord. So, whether we live or **die**, we belong to the Lord" (Romans 14:7-8).

"My dear children, I write this to you so that you will not sin. But if anybody does sin, we have one who speaks to the Father in our defense—Jesus Christ, the Righteous One. He is the atoning sacrifice for our sins, and not only for ours but also for the sins of the whole world" (1 John 2:1-2).

"For he says, 'In the time of my favor I heard you, and in the day of salvation **I helped you.**' I tell you, now is the time of God's favor, now is the day of salvation" (2 Corinthians 6:1, 2).

"Whoever dwells in the shelter of the Most High will rest in the shadow of the Almighty" (Psalm 91:1).

Faith, Hope, and Love

> If I speak in the tongues of men and of angels, but have not **love**, I am only a resounding gong or a clanging cymbal. If I have the gift of prophecy and can fathom all mysteries and all knowledge, and if I have a **faith** that can move mountains, but have not **love**, I am nothing. If I give all I possess to the poor and surrender my body to the flames, but have not **love**, I gain nothing

Love is patient, **love** is kind. It does not envy, it does not boast, it is not proud. It is not rude, it is not self-seeking, it is not easily angered, it keeps no record of wrongs. **Love** does not delight in evil but rejoices with the truth. It always protects, always trusts, always **hope**s, always perseveres.

Love never fails. But where there are prophecies, they will cease; where there are tongues, they will be stilled; where there is knowledge, it will pass away. For we know in part and we prophesy in part, but when perfection comes, the imperfect disappears.

When I was a child, I talked like a child, I thought like a child, I reasoned like a child. When I became a man, I put childish ways behind me. Now we see but a poor reflection as in a mirror; then we shall see face to face. Now I know in part; then I shall know fully, even as I am fully known.

And now these three remain: **faith, hope and love**. But the greatest of these is **love.**

(1 Corinthians 13:1-13).

Plan of Salvation

"Godly sorrow brings repentance that leads to salvation . . . " (2 Corinthians 7:10)

"For he says, 'In the time of my favor I heard you, and in the **day of salvation** I helped you.' I tell you, now is the time of God's favor, **now is the day of salvation**" (2 Corinthians 6:2).

You never have to grieve alone. "Believe in the Lord Jesus, and you will be saved—you and your household" (Acts 16:31), and there will always be someone who cares.

Prayer of Salvation

I believe that Jesus is the Son of God, and that He died for my sins. I'm sorry for my sins. Please forgive me. Come into my heart, and live in me. Save me, cleanse me, and make me one of Your own. In the name of Jesus, God's Son, I pray.

Sign name   Date of conversion

Just one drop of the blood Jesus spilled on the cross will wash away the pain, release all sin and guilt, and grant the ability to move ahead with joy and peace in your heart.

"I will **forgive** their wickedness and will remember their sins no more" (Hebrews 8:12).

"Jesus said, 'You have now seen him; in fact, He is the one speaking with you'" (John 9:37).

Injustices and Forgiveness

"Forgive your brothers the sins and the wrongs they committed in treating you so badly . . . " (Genesis 50:17)

Looking back over a lifetime of injustices, heartache, disappointment, mistakes, regrets, and wrong decisions can make one rethink their objectives and goals. It's important to take account of ourselves and purge our heart of any animosity, bitterness, even hatred, toward others.

Who can recognize our errors? Who can know our hidden thoughts?

"But blessed is the one who trusts in the Lord, whose confidence is in him. They will be like a tree planted by the water that sends out its roots by the stream. It does not fear when heat comes; its leaves are always green. It has no worries in a year of drought and never fails to bear fruit.

The heart is deceitful above all things and beyond cure. Who can understand it? I the Lord search the heart and examine the mind, to reward each person according to their conduct, according to what their deeds deserve" (Jeremiah 17:7-10).

But how do I overcome all the injustices served me over a lifetime?

Forgiveness is the first step in rethinking and redesigning our lives. Mercy for others is essential for healing and forgiveness. First, we must forgive others for the wrongs done against us. Then we must forgive ourselves for harboring hatred and hostility toward them.

"You ought to **forgive** and **comfort** him, so that he will not be overwhelmed by excessive **sorrow**" (2 Corinthians 2:7).

"Bear with each other and **forgive** one another if any of you has a grievance against someone. **Forgive** as the Lord forgave you" (Colossians 3:13**).**

"Even if they sin against you seven times in a day and seven times come back to you saying 'I repent,' you must **forgive** them" (Luke 17:4).

"In him we have redemption through his blood, the forgiveness of sins, in accordance with the riches of God's grace" (Ephesians 1:7).

God's Word will help us find healing and restoration, even in the most difficult of circumstances. Our prayer will be the path to forgiving others who have inflicted harsh wounds into our life.

"If we confess our sins, he is faithful and just and will **forgive** us our sins and purify us from all unrighteousness" (1 John 1:9).

Lastly, after we have forgiven others we must forgive ourselves. Only then will the weight of guilt melt into sheer freedom.

"So if the Son sets you free, you will be free indeed" (John 8:36).

And whatever effort it takes to achieve that freedom will have value beyond measure.

Many prayers had been prayed for Matthew's salvation. In desperation, prayers changed to, "whatever it takes." Be careful how you pray. God may answer your prayer.

CHAPTER TWENTY-FOUR

Fictional Narratives

Another way to grieve is by composing a narrative of relative significance. Your story may have a better ending than the one experienced following the loss of a loved one. Writing fictional stories about similar circumstances was one way of alleviating the painful memories that followed the death of my son.

Often a story will simulate circumstances related to your loss. Other times, the circumstances are changed reflecting a desire for a different outcome. Unique expressions of sorrow may offer an atypical spin concerning a different kind of sorrow. Either way, putting thoughts and feelings on paper can provide yet another facet of healing as you struggle to overcome personal grief and sorrow.

A narrative can be written as a way of addressing the issues of an empty or broken heart. When life throws a curve, it helps to journal those thoughts and feelings, therefore reducing the need to repress emotional distress. Disclosing the facts of your grief with others can help to lessen the pain of sorrow.

Even if the story is fictional, it can aid with the healing process following the death of a loved one. You're not alone. Others around the world are grieving with you.

White Easter

"And we know that in all things God works for the good of those who love him, who have been called according to his purpose" (Romans 8:28).

"Looks like we're having a white Easter this year," Deb said as she stood, hands on hips, while staring outside. The trim around the window framed feathery snowflakes as they cascaded gently to the ground from an overcast sky.

"Alright!" Austin dashed to the window for a quick look outside, raking his hands through his scruffy red hair on the way. "Now we can hunt Easter eggs in the snow!"

"Not so fast," Jim said. He tousled his son's uncombed head after joining him. "We have church this morning before Easter egg hunts."

"Oh yeah, I forgot." Austin scrunched his nose and scratched his head as he watched snow pile up around a thick rock wall just outside the window.

Easter was early this year, coming in March instead of April as it had last year. Daffodils already in bloom next to the wall cast their shadow on the fallen snow. With the return of wintry weather, Easter no longer looked or felt like a spring holiday. The cold air sent chills up his spine every time Austin cracked open the door for a closer look.

After lunch as Austin sat on the sofa reading a comic book, he heard a car door open. "Hey, Mom. Somebody's car just stopped outside."

He jumped down from the sofa and peered through the window. "Look. They're getting out and walking to the house."

A woman in her mid-thirties, holding the hand of a young girl, trudged up the snow-covered walkway. Their shoes left a trail of shimmering footprints behind.

When the doorbell chimed, Austin ran to the door.

"Hello," he said, peering out.

"Hi. My name's Courtney, and this is my little girl Andrea. Our car just broke down, and my cell phone died, so I couldn't call for help. Could I use your phone?"

"Mom ..." Austin's voice trailed. He stepped aside as Deb moved closer to the doorway.

Courtney repeated her request, and she and Andrea were invited inside.

"We've been traveling for two days on our way back to Florida, where we live." Courtney said in a meek voice. "Andrea has leukemia. She had a doctor's appointment in Memphis at the cancer center for kids. But my car broke down, and I don't have any money left to get it fixed. I don't know what I'm going to do."

Deb noted the look of despair on Courtney's face and realized the depth of the situation. "Don't worry about that right now," she said. "Take your jackets off, and have some hot chocolate. We'll figure something out."

"Why are you wearing that?" Austin pointed to a bright pink turban on Andrea's head.

"To hide my head," she said, looking down.

"She has leukemia," Courtney said again. "Her medication makes her hair fall out."

Meanwhile, Jim was outside assessing the car problem. He returned in just minutes with his report.

"You have an oil leak for one thing," he said. "And there seems to be a problem with the engine because it won't turn over. I'm no mechanic, but it's more than a dead battery." He scratched his head. "The car garage is closed until Tuesday because of the holidays."

"Honey, can I talk to you for a minute?" Deb pulled Jim's arm and drew him into the dining room.

"For some reason, I feel like we should offer them a place to stay until Tuesday. She can get her car fixed then. Maybe that's God speaking to me. What do you think?"

"Where would we put them?" Jim asked.

"The spare bedroom's always clean," Deb said.

"Is that what you want to do?" Jim rested his finger on his forehead.

"I feel like that's what God wants us to do." Deb turned on her heel and left the room.

In the living room, Andrea was jumping up and down in excitement. "I've never seen snow before," she said as her eyes twinkled.

"We've always been in Florida," Courtney said. "Memphis is as far as we've ever been from home. It's a long drive."

Deb glanced down at the little girl. "Is the hospital helping her?"

"She's been sick for two years, since she turned three," Courtney's hands were shaking. "We don't know, but we're hoping."

"Can we go outside for a little while?" Andrea asked. "I want to touch the snow again."

"No, Andrea. It's too cold, and you've been sick."

But when Courtney noticed disappointment on Andrea's face, she softened. ""Well, maybe—I guess so—why not?"

In just minutes, Austin, Andrea, and Courtney were bundled up, and walking through the swirling mist of snowflakes.

Austin grabbed a handful of snow. "Let's build a snowman," he said as he formed a ball from the white mixture. He rolled it into a larger sphere to create the base of the snowman. "This is better than hunting Easter eggs any old day," he said with a laugh.

"I know," Andrea said as she handed Austin another handful of the fluffy white stuff.

In record time a gigantic snowman emerged amid the blustery wind and white snowflakes.

Andrea giggled as she helped dress their creation in an orange hat and green-striped scarf.

The next day Courtney stared through the car window one last time as she and Andrea prepared to leave. "I can't thank you enough for everything you've done," she said. "I couldn't get my car fixed, or anything else, without the help of this family. You were a Godsend to us, a miracle."

"I'm just glad we could help." Deb reached through the car window and gave her a quick hug.

Courtney turned the key in the ignition, and slowly backed down the slushy driveway.

"I hope we hear from you again." Deb's voice echoed back as the couple drove away.

Five weeks later, an envelope arrived in the mail. As Deb ripped the seal, a clipped obituary page dropped to the floor. She saw the name 'Andrea' centered at the top of the page.

"Oh, no," she said, putting her hand on her heart. She reached down and scooped up the page as tears formed, and trickled down on the clipping in her hand. A yellow sticky note stuck to the page had a message scribbled in blue ink. It read, *Andrea's best day on earth was playing in the snow.*

Deb wiped away more tears, and shook her head in disbelief. "You never know when you help someone what the outcome will be," she said out loud. "You just never know."

Loner On The Road

"And Jesus … saith unto them, 'Have faith in God' " (Mark 11:22) (KJV).

The sky was dark as Susan gazed out her window one last time before retiring to bed. The hour was late, and the road in front of the home was void of traffic. The only sounds she heard were crickets chirping, and the distant hooting of an owl. With a heavy heart she drew the curtains and closed the door. Falling to her knees, she began to pray for her son. The wayward nineteen-year-old was out there somewhere—but where? Although she hadn't seen or heard from him in days, she had to trust in God. There was no one else.

The next morning, Susan awoke to dazzling rays of sunlight streaming across the room. The month of May was here, and Mother's Day just around the corner. However, the bright sunshine did little to mend her broken heart. What was there to be happy about? She didn't know where her son was, so what good was Mother's Day? Was he safe? Did he have anything to eat?

Susan began each day praying for Jonathan's safe return. At times, she would break down with a steady flow of tears. Other times, she was stolid and firm as she maintained her faith in God.

A very stiff Jonathan crawled out of a makeshift bed of damp leaves and moss. The woods hadn't offered much. His money was gone, and his friends were gone. *What kind of friends where they, anyway?*

He lost his train of thought as his stomach growled. He gripped it to lessen the empty ache inside, and his mind focused on the reason for his hunger. His mouth began to water as an imaginary aroma of bacon and pancakes wafted through his nostrils. Remembering his routine waste of food when living at home, he felt a sudden prick of shame.

He picked up the small plastic bag that contained what was left of his personal belongings, and stumbled out of the woods and onto the road. Maybe he would try to thumb a ride. He just wanted to go home.

He readied himself for the upcoming cars, but the drivers rushed past without a second glance.

After several minutes without any luck, his voice exploded. "No food. No ride. Now what?" Slinging his bag over his shoulder, he tromped along the edge of the road in the direction of the nearest town.

Later that morning, Jonathan stood near an Interstate ramp holding a torn piece of cardboard with the word *Hungry* scribbled on it. He reasoned this was a good place to panhandle. Maybe he would get enough money to purchase a bite to eat at one of those fast food restaurants nearby. Then he would try thumbing again for a ride home. Yes, he had decided it was time to go home. Maybe he would trust God this time and not in himself. A little prayer couldn't hurt.

At that moment, a yellow Tracker stopped at the light, and the lady driver motioned him over. When he reached the window, she handed him a folded piece of money. "This is all I have," she said. "It's just fifteen dollars."

"Wow, thanks." Jonathan grinned as he slipped the money into his pocket. "Thank you. I really appreciate this." Then he gushed, "I'm trying to get home. Pray for me." He felt his face flush red. *Why did I say that?*

"I will," the lady said.

Jonathan stepped back as the light turned green. The lady waved and was gone.

"Fifteen dollars," Jonathan said out loud after counting the money for himself. "That's a lot. Somebody must be looking out for me."

The radiant sun cast shadows on the orange lilies blooming near the rock wall in Susan's flower garden on Mother's Day. Rows of purple and yellow dotted her landscaped yard as she stepped outside.

She thought about the goodness of God as she locked the front door. What a beautiful world she lived in.

Since church was close to her home, Susan decided a brisk walk would be good for her—maybe help clear her mind. She started down the front steps when she noticed a young man trudging down the road. His hair was disheveled, and he needed a shave.

With a loud squeal, Susan dropped her purse and ran toward Jonathan, arms outstretched. "You're home," she said as tears dropped onto her sleeve. "You're home. This is the best present ever."

"Yeah, I'm home," Jonathan said. Then he grinned. "And I don't ever want to leave home again."

"I was so worried," Susan said. "You have no idea how much I've prayed for you. You just don't know."

"Mom, I always knew you were praying." Jonathan squeezed his mother's arm.

"How did you know?" Susan asked.

Jonathan grabbed his mother's hands, and stared into her eyes. "Because when I decided to come home, people I didn't know gave me money for food. Strangers stopped and offered me rides. But more than that—I started believing in your prayers. I remembered things you'd told me about God. Then I started praying myself." He shrugged his shoulders. "Everything just kind of fell into place."

Susan beamed through her tears. "And ..." she said, gazing at her son.

"And . . . I got home." Jonathan gave his mom a squeeze, while grinning from ear to ear.

Brown Paper Bag

A Mother's Day Story

"And we know that all things work together for good to them that love God, to them who are the called according to his purpose" (Romans 8:28 KJV).

Robert wanted a son, but Rachael just wanted a child. She longed to be a mother, to feel the warmth of a child's embrace, and to know the love of a child, no matter the cost.

Following a long struggle of legal procedures, their application to adopt was finally approved, and they were ecstatic. Rachael danced for joy, and Robert snapped a picture as a memento of their achievement.

Rachael felt blessed that three-year-old Trevor's background of being abused and neglected hadn't made him timid or angry. Instead, his appreciation for positive attention kept him busy blowing kisses at her with innocent abandonment. It was obvious he was grateful for a new start in his young life, and she was happy at last to be a mother.

Since Trevor's adoption, Robert and Rachel had been anxious to introduce him to his new grandparents. And Mother's Day seemed the perfect time for this introduction.

As soon as church was dismissed on Sunday morning, they hurried to their car for the two-hour drive. Rachael hummed the words of her favorite song as a brilliant sunshine scattered its dazzling rays through a cloudless sky.

"Let's get some fresh mountain air," Robert said as he rolled his window down.

A wind-blown, wide-eyed Trevor stared longingly through the opening. "Are we there yet?" he asked, an eager look on his face.

"Not yet, but almost." Rachael brushed a few stray hairs from her face. "I know you're excited. It won't be long. Your new grandparents are probably as anxious as you."

As their van rolled into the driveway, Trevor bounced up and down. "Look, just look," he shouted, pointing in the direction of his new grandma's flower garden. "Look at all those flowers!"

Robert lifted Trevor from his car seat as the new grandparents walked over to them.

"Can I pick some? Please, please?" Trevor held both hands under his chin as if praying.

"No, I don't think so, sweetie." Rachael touched Trevor's arm in soft response. "These flowers are your grandma's prized flowers."

Grandma gave Trevor a quick hug. "Today's a special day, and my new grandson may pick as many flowers as he wants. Why don't you pick a special one for your new mommy on Mother's Day?"

Trevor did a flip and squealed in anticipation of his new venture. He sprinted down the rock path that led to the colorful flower garden, and began darting in and out of red roses, yellow jonquils, and purple iris.

"Aren't you growing these flowers for the contest?" Rachael asked her mother.

"That doesn't matter. If it makes him happy, I don't care if he picks them all." Grandma moved closer to Rachael, and whispered in her ear. "I'm glad you adopted him. He's such a delight to watch."

"It's okay for us to spoil him, isn't it?" Grandpa asked.

All of a sudden, Trevor squealed. "I got it! I got the perfect flower for Mommy!"

Ripping through the flower garden, and tripping over jonquils and roses, Trevor raced back to his family. In his grubby little hands was the largest sunflower in the garden, roots, dirt, and all.

"This is for you, Mommy! I got this one just for you!" Panting, and out of breath, the excited boy stopped right in front of his new mother.

Rachael gasped as Trevor, beaming with the pride of youth, thrust an enormous sunflower into her hands, dumping dirt onto her dress as the roots shed their residue.

"It's so big," she said, a little uncertain. But as she held the large plant in her hands, she realized how much Trevor must love her. She reached for him and drew him close, folding her arms around him as if to never let him go. "It's beautiful," she whispered. "I love you so much." Unexpected tears cascaded down her cheeks as she pressed Trevor closer to her heart. "Just look what God did. He made the perfect flower for you to give me on Mother's Day. But better yet, He made *you* just for me."

"I know." Trevor's grubby fingers gently stroked Rachael's arms. "I know."

Robert stepped up with his camera. "We need a picture of this," he said, snapping another image for their photo album.

Rachael tried to smile through glistening tears as she held up a rather large sunflower with a now broken stem for the picture, her small protégé by her side.

On the return trip home, Rachael gazed at Robert as her tears welled up again. "I'll never forget my first Mother's Day," she said. "It was just perfect."

"I agree," Robert said. Full of pride, he glanced at Trevor, asleep in his car seat. "This has been a perfect day—a picture-perfect day."

Seventeen years later, Rachael stood in silence as she examined the contents of the crisp paper bag a kind officer handed her at the scene of a fatal car crash. On the bottom of the sack lay a faded and somewhat weathered wallet. With tender fingers she stroked the smooth texture of aged leather that had softened over time. Lifting the shabby wallet to her face, she breathed in the faint aroma of her son as a wrinkled picture slid silently to the ground. She bent over and picked up the ragged picture of her beloved son as he handed her a rather large sunflower with a broken stem.

CHAPTER TWENTY-FIVE

Mutual Understanding and Condolences

Hi Cathy,

I've been thinking about you all week because I know it's been five years since Dom went away. This is not a celebration—nothing more to celebrate. It's a landmark, a milestone of sorrow. I'll always feel your grief as you feel mine. We're bonded in a sisterhood of sadness, for I know your pain and grieve with you as you grieve with me.

Hi Phoebe,

Thank you so much for your kind words. Whenever another mother talks to me who has lost a child, it's like they're inside my head. You know every emotion and how you go on in your life, but it is never the same. I can now see how people can die of a broken heart because the pain comes and goes and sometimes hits you at a time when you least expect. It just takes you down. Every once in a while the magnitude of Dom's loss hits me, and it takes my breath away. I say to myself, "My God, he's really gone, and I'll never see him in this life again." You can't wrap your head around it.

I sometimes wonder if other mothers, like you, don't really want to talk about it anymore, so I don't bring Dom up as much as I used to. His life is like a good movie that I have to keep replaying because there is no sequel; it's over. My daughter will say, "Remember when Dom did this or that," and that's how we keep him alive in our hearts. A couple of my friends had a mass said for Dom, so we went to that, which was nice, and they also came. What I cannot believe is that my husband's sisters did not call, e-mail, or anything to say they were thinking of him! I know he was hurt as he mentioned it to me. I was aware of it, but didn't want to bring it up. Sometimes family is the most disappointing of all.

Thanks for being there for me. I appreciate it more than you know. It's amazing how people like us, who just happened to come in contact because of our shared sadness, are the kindest of all. I always say I belong to a sad club, and I don't want anymore members.

Take care. Cathy

Hi Phoebe,

Isn't it amazing how the time goes by when you're a parent? One minute they are starting kindergarten, and the next thing you know they want the keys to the car. Sometimes I wish I could live my life in reverse. I'm still appreciative of things in life, but it just never gets back to where it should be when you lose a child. There's always this hole you're trying to fill. Sometimes when we go out to eat, it hits me that we are sitting there, three instead of four. I imagine what it would feel like to have Dom walk through the door and sit with us again. I see Dom's sister, cousins, and friends going on with their lives, and it can't help but sting a little. It will hit me at the oddest times, and I find myself crying. The other day I was in the shower and broke down for no reason at all. Losing a child is a wound that never quite heals.

Cathy

Hi Cathy,

You said it all. The other day when I got home I noticed a young man walking in the distance. He was the same stature as Matthew, looked like him, and was dressed in a similar way. And he was wearing a baseball cap. Matt always wore one. My heart missed a beat. Then that awful feeling hit me in the gut and made me sick. To make matters worse, I was listening to that song by Michael Buble called *Home.* I cried my eyes out. Have you heard that song?

Oh, Phoebe . . . that song by Michael Buble always makes me think of Dom, and it rips me apart!! It's a beautiful song, but sometimes when it comes on the radio, I have to change the channel because I can't handle it. It always makes me think, maybe Dom is looking down on us and wishing he could be here for all the changes that have happened; but, then according to what I've read, they are at perfect peace. I sure wouldn't want him to be looking back and feeling sad. I do wonder though if he misses us at times like we miss him. I wonder, with no time or space, what do you do? Where do you go? What is this afterlife? I can't imagine not having an earthly body to contend with. So many crazy questions go through your head when you lose someone. All we can do is speculate as to what it's like.

It's always good to be able to talk to you like this. It gives me some peace because I know you understand.
Cathy

"Mourn with those who mourn . . . " (Romans 12:15)

The grieving never stops but is enhanced by memories of the past coupled with an unspeakable desire for what could have been but never will be. Broken pieces of the heart can be pieced back together, but it will never be complete and whole. Signs of a shattered heart will expose fractures of accumulated sadness and sorrow because the soul has been crushed beyond repair. It helps to know someone cares.

Several condolences listed online at www.Brigmans.com, the funeral home entrusted with Matthew's memorial service and burial, are worth keeping for future consolation. The sincerity of those comforting words speak volumes of love and concern as their sorrow spills forth in words of sadness over a loss. It's endearing to understand another's perception of your loved one, and to realize how one life can effect so many.

Spending time re-reading cards and mementos will continue to serve as a compassionate reminder that others care about your loss.

Obituary

Stephen Matthew Foley

Stephen Matthew Foley, 22, of Stoneville, North Carolina formally of Black Mountain, North Carolina, died Wednesday, July 28, 2004 at Morehead Memorial Hospital.

He was born on May 10, 1982 in Greensboro, North Carolina, the son of the late Hayman E. Foley, Jr. and Phoebe Ledbetter Foley Leggett, who resides in Charlotte, North Carolina. He was employed by Food Lion of Mayodan, North Carolina.

In addition to his mother, he is survived by his step-father Dana Leggett of Charlotte; sister, Dawn Burnette, husband Shane, and daughter, Samantha of Greenville, South Carolina; brother Brian Foley of Jackson, Tennessee; grandmother, Kathleen Ledbetter of Black Mountain, North Carolina; grandfather Hayman E. Foley, Sr. and wife Norma of Winston-Salem, North Carolina

Online Condolences

This must be the hardest thing you've ever had to go through. My heart can only image the pain. When I lost my baby, a friend sent this comment to me, and I have always remembered it when going through bad things. "God has not always promised that the sky will always be blue. But he does promise to give you the strength to carry you though." You are in my thoughts and prayers. If you need anything call. Matthew was such a bright light in this world. There will always be a dark spot in our hearts without him. Maybe God had a place in heaven that He needed him to brighten.

Our prayers and love are with you.Be strengthened in His love and peace. You know how to get in touch with me if you need to. I'll keep in touch.

We were so saddened to hear the news about Matthew. You will be in our thoughts and prayers every day. Please know we are here if you need anything.

We are praying for you. May God's peace be on you and the family.

I am sorry for the loss of a son, brother, cousin, and friend. Words can never describe the pain that is felt for the loss of Matthew. He will be missed by everyone that ever knew him. I am glad that we were able to be in Matthew's life again, even though for just a short time. I know that the pain in the loss is worth the fulfillment in words that were shared between us. We will always be here. God bless all of you

We have been praying for you and your family and continue to pray for Gods strength and comfort to be with you beyond understanding at this time. I know there are no words that can take the place of a son right now, but when we "look up" we can not be "looking down" at the same time. So let your friends hold you up, and I know you will grow stronger every day as only God can heal the hurt that you feel. Love you

My knowledge of Matt is through his mother Phoebe, who is devastated by this loss. It had appeared that he had a chance for a good life after a period of past difficulty. There were dreams and plans that had a real chance of success. It is tragic that these hopes could not be realized. I sympathize deeply with Mrs. Leggett and all of those who have suffered this loss.

You two are very precious to us, and we want to let you know our hearts and prayers are with you. Your son was a very fine and handsome young man. May the Lord be with you mightily at this time in your life.

We are so sorry to hear of your loss. You will always be in our prayers. Now you will have one more angel in heaven to watch over you.

I don't know you folks, and I don't intend to understand your pain over the loss of your son. I do however want to pray for you and your family, just to let our Lord be praised in all that we do and say. My deepest sympathy goes out to you. God bless you in this time of need.

We send up prayers for the entire family. Our hearts go out to you in your time of loss. Take one day at a time and believe in our Lord JESUS to give you the strength. We were your ex-neighbors on Jadewood and got the news through ConAgra's; and immediately wanted you to know that we are praying. I don't know how you may be feeling, but God knows, and he does care.

Please know your family is in our prayers. I pray for strength and comfort for your loss. Phoebe, the good memories will help you through the hard times. Blessings to you.

It's hard for me to put this into words . . . Matt was a friend of mine and a good one. No matter how bad the day was, he had a joke or something to say to make me laugh. I've been blessed to know Matt. I never saw him angry, and he was kind to everyone he'd meet. I think that I and Matt's friends here could learn a lot through the way he was. I don't have a bad memory of Matt, and I would like to say I'm very sorry for your loss. He loved his family very much. If there is anything I can do, even if it is as simple as a phone call, let me know.

This is my second hardest thing to have to go through besides my own grandmother's death. What I feel is something I just can't start to tell. Matt left my house that night to go to Taco Bell to get a couple of tacos, and never came back. He was planning to stay that night, but never came back.

We had just finished watching a movie, and he wanted some tacos, so he decided to go to Madison and get him a few. But never came back.
I have a hard time dealing with this sometimes. I really thought that maybe if I had made him eat something I had, or even gone with him out to eat, this might not have happened. This has really hurt me that no one can imagine what I have felt in the past month. But one thing I do know, when GOD is ready, there is nothing anyone on this earth can choose to do. They can't take another path.I know that Matt had really changed since his time with my mom, and I hope that before his death, he had the chance to make sure with our Lord that his life was right with GOD. I believe this happened and hope and pray that his death will show others that no matter what you go through, there is an almighty God that loves us. Our hearts go out to all who knew him.

May the peace of Christ rule in your heart. May God grant you the serenity and restoration to you and family that only He can provide. Love never fails.

Wow! I don't even know where to begin! Matthew was one of a kind, that's for sure. He could drive you crazy, but would be the one to come through for you in your time of need. Growing up next door to the Foley's was a blessing. Having the Foley's as neighbors sure made my childhood memorable. It just blows my mind when I think how little we were and how time flies, and we lose touch of our youthfulness and don't cherish every second of everyday. That's what I loved about Matthew. He was so happy-go-lucky, and all he wanted to do was make everyone laugh and have a ball! Matthew had a good heart and a free spirit. One of my favorite memories of Matthew is when my parents left me at home on my b-day alone and he felt sorry for me, so he walked to Food Lion, bought me a small cake, and gave me one of his mom's potted plants! We were very young at the time . . . it makes me laugh every time I think about it! He just loved to see people happy. He was a very selfless person. He was a true servant of God. I'm not worried. I know that one day I'll see Matthew again, and I will be able to thank him for all the fun times he gave to me!"I fought a good fight, I have finished the race, and I have remained faithful" (2 Timothy 4:7).

I am truly sorry for your loss. My wife and I, along with our staff, will be praying for you and your family. Keep the faith. In Him, 3 John 2

I am so sorry to hear about the loss of your loved one. Things will get better in time, just have to have faith. You'll see him again, when it's your time. God needed him for something that was important to him.

We are so very saddened by the death of Matthew. He was a delightful young man. We never know why or how things happen. All of our thoughts and prayers are with you always.

We just wanted you and the family to know that you are in our prayers. Please know how sorry we are over your loss.

My sympathies and sincere prayers are with you at the loss you've endured. I feel blessed that I got to know Matthew. He always was a joy to be around, and I enjoyed our times together. He always made me laugh, so while I grieve at the thought of not seeing Matthew on earth again, I celebrate his life on earth and the people he touched. I had the privilege of spending a Christmas with him, Brian, Dana, and Phoebe. He made me feel very welcomed and at home. God bless you, Matthew.

CHAPTER TWENTY-SIX

Moving Forward

At some point after the death of a loved one, the harshness of sorrow will soften, but it may take months, even years, before that can happen. It's best to allow whatever amount of time is needed to process the details of your loss. The course may be difficult to maneuver, but peace and happiness will come again. Sorrow and pain are but for a season, as God desires each of us to live our lives to the fullest.

"Weeping may endure for a night but joy comes in the morning" (Psalm 30:5 KJV).

Without a doubt, trials and death are part of the sequence. Losing a loved one will be difficult, if not impossible, to accept for a time. Many have said they will carry their sorrow to the grave. It's expected that a parent will pass when they are old. It's understandable that a spouse will one day die. But it's not reasonable for a parent to outlive a child.

Having to deal with the death of someone you hold dear will eventually happen. When that moment comes, allow God to be your traveling companion. With His help and the help of others, the hurdle of grief can be overcome with grace and peace in your heart.

CONCLUSION

End of the Road

"Come to me, all you who are weary and burdened, and I will give you rest. Take my yoke upon you and learn from me, for I am gentle and humble in heart, and you will find rest for your souls" (Matthew 11:28, 29).

I had been told many times that I need healing. To be cured from despair, anger, and my many hurts. But I wasn't receptive. The hurt was just too deep. After all, I was the one who was in control. I could handle it. Those offenses were part of who I was.

Medicine hadn't worked. Well, it helped for the short haul. But long term, it was just another crutch—an addiction without a cure.

I was tired. I was weary. And my strength was almost gone. My will to live was dying too. That never-ending road ahead was full of curves and potholes. I was just too worn out for the journey.

What could I do now? I was at the end of the road, ready to jump off a bridge and end it all, to be done with my life. What was left for me? I was out of options.

Stuck in a rut, weathered and exhausted, I struggled with my decision.

As a last resort, I picked up the Bible. When I opened the book, words of restoration leaped off the page and into my spirit. "Come to me, all you who are weary and burdened, and I will give you rest" (Matthew 11:28). What did that mean? Reading further, I found the answer.

Give the depression, the sorrow, and the heartache to God. Release the pain, the hurt, and the anger. Let go of all bitterness, and allow the burden of grief to rest on the shoulders of the One who's big enough to carry it.

"You will not have to fight this battle. Do not be afraid; do not be discouraged. For the battle is not yours, but God's . . . " (2 Chronicles 20:17, 15).

Set it free, give it to God, and let it go.
And I did.

"He who dwells in the shelter of the Most High will rest in the shadow of the Almighty" (Psalm 91:1).

The End

Credits

Grieving God's Way by Margaret Brownley
Mourning and Melancholia (1917), Sigmund Freud
After a Child Dies by Harold K. Bush, Jr.
Drawings by Matthew Foley
www. phoebe-leggett.com

Bibliography

Mourning and Melancholia (1917) Sigmund Freud Freud, Sigmund. (1916-1917g [1915]) "Trauer und Melancholie," *Intern. Zschr. ärztl. Psychoanal 4*, p. 277-287; *G.W.*, 10, 428-448; Mourning and melancholia. *SE*, 14: 243-258.

Some information obtained from Stages of Grieving, Grieving God's Way ©.Copyright 2004 Margaret Brownley. WinePress Publishing, January 2004
Zondervan Bible New International Version Copyright 1973, 1978, 1984 by International Bible Society® The Zondervan Corporation Grand Rapids, MI 49530 U.S.A.
New International Version, ©2011 ***(NIV)*** Copyright © 1973, 1978, 1984, 2011 by Biblica

"It Is Well with My Soul" *Words:* Horatio G. Spafford, 1873. *Music:* Ville du Havre, Philip P. Bliss, in *Gospel Hymns No. 2*, by P. P. Bliss & Ira D. Sankey (New York: Biglow & Main, 1876), number 76 (*note:* published in a combined volume with the 1875 *Gospel Hymns and Sacred Songs*) (MIDI, NWC, PDF). Ironically, Bliss himself died in a train wreck shortly after writing this music.

Dictionary.com, LLC. Copyright © 2011 www.dictionary.com

Scarlett O'Hara, a character from Margaret Mitchell's 1936 novel *Gone With the Wind.* The book was first published in 1936 by the Macmillan Company in New York

Grief Resources

http://www.griefshare.org/
http://grief.net/
http://www.missionsinternational.org/store.htm
Andrew Wommack, www.awmi.net
Ann Tatlock—www.anntatlock.com
Brigman's Funeral Home, www.brigmans.com—funeral home that serviced our family
Billy Graham's *The Cove* (800) 950-2092 or visit www.thecove.org. Billy Graham Training Center
Cheryl Salem, www.salemfamilyministries.org
http://www.missionsinternational.org/store.htm 1-888-710-7706
Del Way, http:www.delway.org
Grief Share, www.griefshare.org—help in finding a location in your area that offers help for grief recovery
Deborah Morocco Mason, Author of *He Held My Hand.*
www.missionsinternational.org
Edie Melson, Editor of Southeast Zone Newsletter and staff reviewer for *Afictionado* magazine www.thewriteconversation.blogspot.com.
Lifetouch Prestige Portraits
Ray Funeral Home, 119 North Market Street, Madison, NC 27025, (336) 548-9606,
info.ray@forbisanddick.com or www.forbisanddick.com
Rev. Ralph Shelton—Pentecostal Holiness Church evangelist, deceased 2007
Vonda Skelton—Author of *Seeing Through the Lies: Unmasking the Myths Women Believe* and *The Bitsy Burroughs Mysteries.* www.VondaSkelton.com
Yvonne Lehman, Founder of Lifeway Blue Ridge Mountains Christian Writer's Conference, Ridgecrest, North Carolina; director of Blue Ridge "Summer" and "Autumn" novel retreats and author of fifty novels. www.yvonnelehman.com

Contributors

Brian Foley
Carolyn Knefely—Speaker, etiquette specialist and career coach, people polisher and co-director of Christian Communicators www.teacupliving.blogspot.com
Lori Marett—Co-founder Gideon Film Festival—www.gideonfilmfestival.com
Cathy Pendola
Cindy Sproles—Christian Devotions Ministries, P. O. Box 6494, Kingsport TN 37663, christiandevotions.us, www.iBegat.com, DevoKids.com, www.DevoFest.com, devocionescristiano.com, blogtalkradio.com/Christian-Devotions
Ann Tatlock—Novelist and Author of the award winning Christy award, *All the Way Home*. www.anntatlock.com
Belle Woods—www.bellwoods.blogspot.com

Abbreviations

AS Asperger Syndrome
MS Multiple Sclerosis

Now I lay me down to sleep. I pray the Lord my soul to keep.

"May God give you of **heaven**'s dew and of earth's richness . . . " (Genesis 27:28).

Rest in Peace.

www.phoebe-leggett.com

CPSIA information can be obtained at www.ICGtesting.com
Printed in the USA
LVOW060025161111
255142LV00001B/7/P

9 781462 706228